# FOUNDATIONS OF MODERN HISTORY

General Editor A. Goodwin

Professor of Modern History, The University of Manchester

*In the* FOUNDATIONS OF MODERN HISTORY *Series*

I. R. Christie  •  *Crisis of Empire: Great Britain and the American Colonies 1754–1783*
J. R. Jones  •  *Britain and Europe in the Seventeenth Century*
S. H. Steinberg  •  *The  Thirty Years War  and the Conflict for European Hegemony 1600–1660*
Further titles to be announced

FOUNDATIONS OF MODERN HISTORY

# The Thirty Years War
### and the conflict for European hegemony 1600–1660

## by S. H. STEINBERG

W · W · NORTON & COMPANY · INC ·
NEW YORK

# General Preface

In this volume Mr. Steinberg reorientates and reinterprets those complex but momentous upheavals in the heart of seventeenth-century Europe which historians have traditionally, but not very felicitously, labelled the Thirty Years War. He rightly insists that this description is misleading in a double sense – firstly, because it imparts a fictitious unity to conflicts which proliferated rather than escalated from separate regional disputes in different parts of Europe and were never restricted to Germany and secondly, because the Thirty Years War was only a part of the prolonged Bourbon-Habsburg contest for European hegemony which underlay a period of intermittent warfare beginning, not in 1618 but in 1609 and ending, not in 1648 but in 1659. If we are to understand the major displacements of political power in Europe in the seventeenth century – the decline of Spain and the recession of Imperial authority, the independence of the United Provinces, the short-lived ascendancy of Sweden, the preponderance of France and the emergence of Brandenburg-Prussia and Russia – we must, as Mr. Steinberg implies, not confine our attention to the period 1618–48, but attempt to follow the ramifications of political and religious conflict from the disputes over the Jülich-Berg succession to the termination of the Franco-Spanish war at the treaty of the Pyrenees.

The familiar 'myth' of the Thirty Years War, as the author makes clear, was the creation initially of contemporary propagandists and of later publicists. It was given a wider currency by literary or popular historians. It survived even the researches of modern economic historians, who were the first to impugn its validity, and it is significant that the cataclysmic interpretation of the effects of the war on the economic and cultural development of Germany was only challenged by recent historians in consequence of the still greater devastation of the two world wars, followed by the 'economic miracle' of the German Federal Republic. The historical realities of the Thirty Years War and its impact on the religious, political and economic life of Germany can now, however, be depicted, as here, in a way that robs the 'myth' of its exaggerations and enables us to gain a more informed insight into the motives and importance of such

*General Preface*

controversial figures as Gustavus Adolphus and Wallenstein. Mr. Steinberg's final assessment of the meaning of this crisis in the history of seventeenth-century Germany will thus be found acceptable and convincing, not only because it reflects the progress of recent scholarship but also because of its own independent merits and evaluations.

# *Maps*

# Contents

Europe about 1610

Limit of the Holy Roman Empire
Spanish possessions
Austrian possessions
Denmark-Norway
Sweden

1 Holstein
2 United Provinces
3 Guelph Duchies
4 Brandenburg
5 Saxony
6 Silesia
7 Bohemia
8 Franche Comté
9 Bavaria
10 Switzerland
11 Savoy
12 Milan
13 Papal States
14 Estonia
15 Spanish Netherlands
16 Luxembourg

# Introduction

THE term 'Thirty Years War', as applied to the struggle for European hegemony in the first half of the seventeenth century is as much a 'figment of retrospective imagination' as is the label 'Wars of the Roses' affixed to the dynastic civil wars of fifteenth-century England.* The undeniable convenience of both terms, however, together with their deeply-rooted, though erroneous, emotional associations, will probably defy all attempts to relegate either of them to the realms of journalism and fiction.

The traditional interpretation of the origins, course and significance of the so-called Thirty Years War requires no elaboration. According to this version the war began with the Bohemian revolt in 1618 and ended with the peace of Westphalia in 1648. It was, so we have been taught, initially a war of religion between the German Protestants and Catholics, which the foreign powers of Spain, France, Denmark and Sweden exploited, each for political reasons of its own. In this way Germany became the battlefield of Europe for thirty consecutive years. The war completely ruined Germany's economic and intellectual life and left behind it a depopulated, devastated and impoverished country which, for two hundred years, suffered from its disastrous after-effects. The war itself has been regarded as 'the outstanding example in European history of meaningless conflict'.† It is on these views (or a selection of them) that most Germans have been reared during the past century and a half and which British and American scholars have accepted more or less uncritically.

Such a presentation, however, does not conform to historical realities. The Thirty Years War was never exclusively, or even primarily, a German affair but concerned the whole of Europe. It was, to some extent, a by-product of France's efforts, after the conclusion of her religious war, to break her encirclement by the Habsburg powers of Spain and Austria. What happened was that some regions of Germany, but never the whole Empire, inter-mittently took an active part in, or were drawn into, the various hot and cold wars and the diplomatic and ideological conflicts

*S. B. Chrimes, *Lancastrians, Yorkists and Henry VII* (London, 1964), preface.
†C. V. Wedgwood, The Thirty Years War (Penguin edition 1957), p. 460.

I

between the houses of Bourbon and Habsburg. This involvement was dictated by the inescapable fact of Germany's central geographical situation on the European continent and by the intricacies of Habsburg dynastic interests. This larger struggle for European hegemony between Bourbon and Habsburg lasted from 1609 to the peace of the Pyrenees in 1659. Even in Germany proper the series of hostilities, misnamed the Thirty Years War, though terminated by the peace of Westphalia, began, not in 1618, but in 1609.

The determining context of the half-dozen major and half-dozen minor wars of this period was not the religious antagonism between German Protestants and Catholics but rather certain constitutional issues within the Empire which had been germinating during the previous half century. These problems had been raised, on the one hand, by the attempt of the emperor to transform the loose confederation of several hundreds of principalities and free cities into a homogeneous unit under his effective authority and, on the other, by the efforts of most rulers, including the Emperor in his capacity as archduke of Austria and king of Bohemia, to crush their medieval Estates and establish monarchical absolutism. These political struggles were accompanied, overlaid and crossed by ideological conflicts between the adherents of the Roman Catholic, Lutheran and Calvinistic churches. As religion was still the pivot of men's political thoughts and social activities, and as even secular ideas found expression most commonly in biblical and ecclesiastical language, arguments of statecraft and political propaganda readily appeared in the guise of religious or theological controversy. There is no doubt, however, that all· decisions of consequence were taken in the cool light of what at the time became known as *raison d'état*.

Nor were the wars of the seventeenth century any more physically destructive or morally degrading in their effects than other wars before or since. Owing to lack of money and difficulties of supply, all the campaigns were of short duration. The armies involved were comparatively small, averaging each the strength of a modern division. The main theatres of war were those few regions which have, since Roman times, borne the brunt of invasion. As in every such war the open country and its inhabitants suffered most; the majority of the fortified towns never saw an enemy within their walls. The fable of wholesale ruin and misery must therefore be replaced by the less spectacular recognition that between 1600 and 1650 there took place in Germany a redistribution of populations and fortunes, which benefited some regions, places and persons and harmed others. Some of these changes can be attributed to the effects of war but others happened independently of any warlike operation. In 1648 Germany was neither better nor worse off than in 1609: she was simply different from what she had been half a century earlier.

# CHAPTER ONE

# Background and Problems

## Western Europe

*France and Spain.* From the end of the fifteenth to the middle of the seventeenth century France was engaged in a defensive, often desperate struggle against her encirclement by the house of Habsburg. This aspect of European history has been overlaid by the subsequent wars of aggression waged by Louis XIV, the French Revolution and Napoleon I.

The pressure upon France began when in 1477 the archduke Maximilian of Austria, soon to become the Emperor Maximilian I, married the heiress of Charles the Bold of Burgundy and thereby, together with his patrimonial possessions, lined almost the whole northern and eastern frontiers of France with a chain of Habsburg lands and fortresses, from Dunkirk, Cambrai, Luxembourg, Belfort, Besançon and ending just outside Geneva.

The encirclement of France became virtually complete when in 1516 Charles, Maximilian's grandson, inherited through his mother the kingdom of Spain and its vast possessions overseas and in Europe. Here, Spain at the time ruled over the county of Roussillon north of the Pyrenees, the kingdoms of Sardinia, Sicily and Naples and (from 1535) the duchy of Milan in Italy, as well as a number of outposts along the coast of North Africa. On Maximilian's death (1519) Charles obtained also the Burgundian and Austrian dominions of his grandfather and in the same year was elected Holy Roman Emperor – the candidate whom he defeated was King Francis I of France.

The Habsburg ring round France was closed when in 1553 Philip, Charles's heir apparent, married Mary I of England and thereby turned the Tudor kingdom into a Spanish satellite. However, in these very years, the strangulation of France was beginning to relax. In 1556, Charles abdicated and divided his realm among his son Philip II and his brother Ferdinand I. Philip received Spain and her dependencies to which the Netherlands had been assigned some years earlier, while Ferdinand obtained the Austrian lands to which he himself had earlier added the crowns of Bohemia and Hungary. Despite the close ties which the two Habsburg lines maintained with each other, the split could hardly fail to ease the French position.

The earliest indications of the decline of Spanish power – the dissolution of the Anglo-Spanish marriage alliance through the early death of Mary (1558), the rebellion of the Spanish Moors (1566), the revolt of the Netherlands in the same year, and the defeat of the Spanish Armada (1588) – could, however, not be exploited by France. For from 1562 until 1596 France was torn by civil wars, kindled and nourished by religious antagonism, dynastic ambition, opposing political, social and economic objectives – and one party or another was always anxious to appease Spain as an ally against its domestic adversaries. It was only when Henry of Navarre, with English and German support, had decisively defeated the pro-Spanish League and, through his conversion to Roman Catholicism, achieved general recognition as king of France, that the house of Bourbon was in a position to break the Spanish stranglehold. Henry at once declared war upon Spain (1595) and concluded an alliance with England and the Netherlands against the common enemy. The war, however, went badly for France and Henry availed himself gladly of the Pope's offer of mediation. The peace of Vervins (2 May 1598) proved a diplomatic victory for Henry: in return for abandoning his English and Dutch allies. Spain restored to him all the conquered places including Calais. In addition, Philip formally renounced his claim to the French crown. When he died a few months after Vervins, he must have cherished the belief that he had at last secured France's support against his main enemies, England and the Netherlands.

For at sea, Spain had suffered some setbacks. The English attacks on Cadiz and the Azores at least prevented the sailing against England of a second Armada, and the Dutch established their first settlement in Java, thereby successfully breaking the Spanish–Portuguese monopoly of the spice-trade. Above all, the Anglo-Dutch superiority at sea endangered the passage of Spanish reinforcements against the rebellious Netherlands and obliged Spain to secure an alternative route. This was to become a primary concern of Spanish policy and largely explains the Spanish actions during the next fifty years.

In any case, Henry IV was far from abandoning his anti-

Spanish policy. In 1601 he forced Savoy, lately Spain's ally, to cede the district west of the river Rhone, which safeguarded the approaches to Lyon, separated Savoy from the Spanish Franche-Comté and increased French influence in the neighbouring Swiss cantons, the free city of Geneva and the duchy of Savoy. While Henry here threatened the Spanish position in Milan, he shortly afterwards made a direct thrust against the Spanish Netherlands: the duke of Bouillon, whose country straddled the French–Belgian frontier, was forced to admit a French garrison in the strong fortress of Sedan on the Meuse.

The temporary ease which Spain obtained in the Netherlands by the armistice with the United Provinces (9 April 1609) and the prospects of Spain gaining a foothold on the lower Rhine through her intervention in the quarrel about the succession in Jülich-Cleves (April–June), led to the conclusion of an offensive alliance between France, England and the Netherlands (17 June), which was later joined by Savoy and the Protestant Union. Henry was on the point of launching a triple attack against Milan, on the Meuse and on the lower Rhine, when he was assassinated (14 May 1610). The regency council, embarrassed by the renewed flare-up of aristocratic and religious revolts, had to modify the aggressive policy of Henry IV. It was only after the subjection of the rebellious Huguenots and magnates (1629–30) that France, guided by the genius of Richelieu, could again take up the struggle against the house of Habsburg.

Endowed with the hindsight of the mid-twentieth century, we know that the Spain of Philip III (1598–1621) was past its prime. Although 'the legend of the defeat of the Spanish Armada' has become more important than 'the actual event',* there can be no doubt that Spanish seapower was never to recover its pristine glory. The foundation of the English, Dutch and French East India Companies in 1600, 1602 and 1604 respectively showed that colonial expansion and world trade was slipping away from the Iberian peninsula. The temporary incorporation of Portugal (1580–1640) added no real strength to Spanish manpower or economy: it rather widened the possible targets of English, French and Dutch naval enterprises. It was during this period that the Dutch captured the north-east coast of Portuguese Brazil and the Portuguese settlements in Ceylon; and it was on Portuguese soil that Drake, in May 1587, made sure that the Armada

*G. Mattingly, *The Defeat of the Spanish Armada* (London 1961), epilogue.

would be hamstrung by lack of preserved provisions.* The truce of 1609 with the United Provinces can now be seen as the end of Spanish rule in the northern Low Countries; all her subsequent efforts were, as it turned out, doomed to failure. Not thus, however, did the Spanish monarchy appear to contemporary foreign observers. To them, the Spanish monarchy was still the greatest power of the Christian world. The naval victory of Lepanto (1571) gained under Spanish leadership, had smashed Turkish sea-power for good. The younger branch of the house of Habsburg, resident at Vienna, could be considered dependable vassals of the court of Madrid. The most active and successful force of the Catholic Church, the Jesuit Order, was as much at the command of the king of Spain as of that of its nominal head, the Pope. The Spanish treasure fleet, though occasionally inter-cepted by the English seadogs, replenished annually the Spanish exchequer with the gold of Peru, the silver of Mexico and the pearls and spices of the Indies – and the economists found no explanation of the repeated bankruptcies of the Spanish crown (1557, 1575, 1596, 1607) in spite of this flow of bullion and precious merchandise. Nor could it be clear to contemporary students of affairs that the expulsion of the Moriscos (1609–11) was to ruin Spanish agriculture beyond recovery.

The eventual reconquest of the rebellious Dutch provinces was assumed or feared by most contemporaries; they regarded the truce of 1609 merely as a temporary cessation of hostilities, especially as in 1604 England, hitherto the most reliable, if not always the most efficient, ally of the Netherlands had made her peace with Spain and during the following twenty years did her utmost to appease Madrid. The beheading of Sir Walter Raleigh (1618), the abandonment of James I's son-in-law (1619–22) and the attempt to obtain a Spanish bride for the Prince of Wales (1623) could not fail to give the impression that English policy was subservient to the wishes of Madrid.

The Spanish army, especially its infantry, was justifiably regarded as the most efficient and powerful military machine of the age. Forged by one of the greatest captains of the sixteenth century, Alessandro Farnese (1545–92), and kept up to standard by his disciples, among whom the Genoese Ambrogio Spinola (1569–1630) was the most outstanding, the Spanish infantry proved a perfect instrument in their hands. It was recruited mainly

*Mattingly, chapter XI: Barrel staves and treasure.

from the Walloon population of the southern Netherlands and the Lombards of northern Italy; its tactical strength lay in the 'walking citadels' of their closely massed squares, flanked by squadrons of heavy cavalry. Their superiority was broken when Maurice of Orange, from 1590 to his death in 1625 the commander-in-chief of the Dutch forces, introduced a number of epoch-making innovations in the art of war, of which the organization of smaller, mobile combat units and the use of concentrated artillery fire were the most important; Gustavus Adolphus of Sweden and, later, Oliver Cromwell were Maurice's zealous and successful pupils.

*The Netherlands.* For the seven 'United Provinces' of the northern Low Countries the term 'Thirty Years War' has even less significance than for any other European country. Dutch historians and the Dutch people rightly speak of the 'Eighty Years War', which was forced upon the seventeen provinces in 1568 and terminated by the peace signed in Münster on 30 January 1648 by those seven provinces which had survived the Spanish attempts to reconquer the whole Netherlands. What the brutality of Alba's rule (1567–73) failed to achieve, the military genius of Alessandro Farnese brought about, if only partly. At Arras on 17 May 1579, the southern provinces, where the rebellion had originated, again recognized Philip II as their lawful sovereign. When on 26 July 1581 the north formally renounced allegiance to Spain, the division became final into what subsequently became the kingdoms of the Netherlands and of Belgium. Contrary to beliefs long cherished in the north as well as the south of the Low Countries, the frontier has no linguistic, religious or economic foundation or significance; it originally corresponded to the line which the northward drive of the Spanish troops had reached when, in 1609, Spain concluded a truce with the unconquered provinces which were treated 'as if they were' a sovereign republic. Later on, in 1648, the Republic obtained some extension southward, but again with regard only to the military considerations, this time in favour of the north.

The southern Spanish Netherlands, which included Luxembourg but excluded the prince-bishopric of Liège, continued to be ruled by Spanish viceroys resident in the old Burgundian capital of Brussels. In 1596 Philip II entrusted the government to his Austrian nephew, Albert (1559–1621), who had been educated in Madrid, raised to the cardinalate at the age of seventeen, and

had proved his abilities as viceroy of Portugal. Philip even ceded
the Netherlands nominally to his eldest daughter, Isabel, whom
he married to Albert in 1599. As the marriage remained childless, the country reverted on Albert's death to his nephew Philip
IV. From the Spanish point of view, the Netherlands could 'not
have been in better hands: Albert and Isabel completed the re-
catholicization of the southern provinces and gave unstinted
support to their general, Spinola. Spinola in 1605 made some
conquests in the eastern parts of the rebellious north, in 1609 took
the fortress of Wesel in the war of the Jülich succession, in 1617
made the Austrian court promise the cession of Alsace to Spain,
and in 1620 occupied the Palatinate, thus preparing everything
for the resumption of hostilities after the expiry in 1621 of the
twelve-year truce.

The conclusion of this truce with the United Provinces in
1609 was a great diplomatic success for Albert, brought about at
the moment when Henry IV was preparing his onslaught on
Spain; with the United Provinces still in arms, the southern
Netherlands might have been crushed between the two allies. The
assassination of the French king removed this danger, and Albert
was preparing for the resumption of the struggle.

It was too late. By the end of the Eighty Years War the commercial and maritime preponderance of Spain had passed to the
Dutch Republic which had also become a leading colonial
power. Her influence in world affairs was based on her ever-
growing wealth as well as the gifted leadership of the house of
Orange. Nominally the prince, under the title of *Stadholder*, was
only the first magistrate of the confederated republics. Nevertheless, William I (assassinated in 1584) and his sons Maurice (Stadholder 1584–1625) and Frederick Henry (Stadholder 1625–47)
occupied a quasi-monarchical position by sheer force of personality. For the constitution of the United Provinces was deliberately
designed to thwart monarchical as well as centralized tendencies.
Even the States-General could not act on their own but were
entirely dependent on the decisions and instructions which their
members were given by the Estates of each Province. Of the
provinces, Holland with its capital Amsterdam, outdid the rest
in wealth, energy, power and radical republican and religious
sentiment. Contrary to popular legend, the regime was anything
but democratic; all economic and political power was concentrated in the hands of the small oligarchy of the 'regents' whose

administrative head, the 'advocate', later called 'grand-pensionary', equalled the influence of the Stadholder. William the Silent had worked in concert with the 'regents'; the 'advocate' Jan van Oldenbarnevelt was the staunch supporter of Maurice; young Hugo Grotius, one of the 'regents', in 1610 published a spirited defence of the happy mixture of monarchy, aristocracy and democracy which made the United Provinces the fulfilment of Aristotle's criteria of a well-ordered state. By this time, however, the harmony between the Stadholder and the aristocratic faction had begun to break down. The conclusion of the truce with Spain was Oldenbarnevelt's work, which Maurice bitterly opposed; in the burning question of church government and the relationship between state and church – both closely connected with the problem of peace or war – the regents followed a less rigid and more conciliatory course, whereas the Stadholder, fully supported by the religiously strict and politically bellicose middle and lower classes, championed radical measures. The victory eventually lay with Maurice: Grotius was imprisoned and later exiled, Oldenbarnevelt was executed, and the synod of Dort – while laying down the most narrow rules of what constituted Calvinist orthodoxy – tamely submitted control of the church to the secular power (1618–19). Although Maurice missed the opportunity of reforming the cumbersome machinery of the United Provinces, their political and commercial interests pointed clearly in the direction of supporting every anti-Habsburg movement, whether championed by the Bohemian nobility, the German princes or the crowns of France and Sweden.

*Italy.* Spain's most vulnerable flank was surprisingly Italy. More than half of the peninsula, it is true, was Spanish territory proper – Naples, Sicily, Sardinia, Milan – and some of the petty princes, such as the Gonzaga of Mantua, the Este of Ferrara and Modena, as well as the republic of Genoa, and even the Medici grand-dukes of Tuscany, could be included in the calculations of the Madrid cabinet as fairly dependable. However, the three most important states of northern and central Italy were far from being amenable to Spanish persuasion or bribery. The most powerful of them – Venice – was in fact the most determined opponent of the Habsburg regime. The ancient 'queen of the Adria' was still one of the richest commercial and financial centres of the world, equally renowned for the quality of her painters, architects

and musicians, the medical and scientific achievements of the
state university of Padua, and the brilliance of her diplomacy.
Hemmed in by the Austrian provinces of Goricia, Carinthia and
Tirol in the east and north, the Spanish duchy of Milan in the
west and the Spanish clienteles of Mantua and Ferrara in the
south, Venice was the natural ally of every anti-Habsburg
government and combination. Her ecclesiastical policy, too,
brought Venice into conflict with the counter-reformation
tendencies of the Habsburg and the Curia. In 1605 the acquisition of landed property by the church and the foundation of
monasteries and churches were subjected to governmental
approval; in the following year the Jesuits were expelled and
Paolo Sarpi, General of the Servite Order, was encouraged to
publish his anti-papal *History of the Council of Trent* and appointed
state adviser of church affairs. Hence collaboration with Henry
IV, Savoy, the Swiss and German Protestants followed for
political as well as ideological reasons.

Less clear-cut was the position of the duchy of Savoy-Piedmont.
Surrounded by France in the west, Milan in the east, Genoa in
the south, and free from pressure only in the north where the
Swiss Confederation was their neighbour, the dukes were torn
by fear of both Spain and France and had perforce to lean now
towards the one now towards the other. Duke Emmanuel I
(1580–1630), taught by the unfortunate result of his short alliance
with Spain (which cost him the north-western part of his country)
and driven by ambition to seek compensations elsewhere, chose the
anti-Habsburg side in the Bohemian and Mantuan wars – thus remaining at least an irritant thorn in the Spanish position in Italy.

For the sea-route from Spain to the southern Netherlands could
easily be interrupted by hostile English, French and Dutch
privateers even in times of nominal peace. Supplies of men,
money, equipment and provisions had therefore to be shipped to
Genoa and thence transported to Milan and across the Alpine
passes by land. This route was threatened by Savoy and Venice
and could be closed by the Grisons – hence the disproportionate
importance of the small republic of the Grisons in European
power-politics.

The third Italian power that caused disquiet to the Spanish
government was the Papal States. The attitude of the Roman
Pontiff was largely determined by his double position as the
spiritual head of the universal church and as the temporal ruler

of central Italy. Which of the two dignities would influence papal policy was unpredictable. As a secular prince, the Pope was intimidated by, as well as dependent upon, his southern neighbour, the Spanish kingdom of Naples. No doubt, Spain was the most zealous protagonist of the counter-reformation which was to restore papal supremacy over the whole Christian world. But was it actually in the interest of the Church that its victory should be entirely due to this one power? Sixtus V was the first post-Tridentine pope to doubt the value of this one-sided connexion. In 1590 he received the ambassadors of Henry of Navarre and Elizabeth of England, and a Saxon envoy was on his way to Rome when Sixtus died (27 August). The disgust with which the Spaniards followed these moves made them exert themselves in forcing upon the cardinals the successive election of three candidates devoted to the Spanish cause – but the three died within little more than a year, and the next pope, Clement VIII (1592–1605), resumed the policy of loosening the Spanish connexion. The absolution given to Henry IV (17 December 1595) established papal independence in the European field; it was French support which enabled Clement to oust the pro-Spanish heir of Ferrara and to incorporate Ferrara in the Papal States (1598); and it was Clement who mediated the peace of Vervins between France and Spain (1598) and the agreement of Lyon between France and Savoy (1600), both favourable to France. In 1604 the college of cardinals again included for the first time for a century a strong French party.

The balance of power within the Catholic world allowed Paul V (1605–21) to give his attention and support to the advance of Catholicism all over Europe. He even could afford to put up with the anti-curial policy of Venice, to wink at the provocation offered by the Elector of Bavaria and the Austrian Habsburgs who imprisoned the archbishop of Salzburg (1611) and the cardinal-bishop of Vienna (1612). The Curia helped to finance the Habsburg in the Bohemian war and persuaded Spain to resume hostilities in the Netherlands after the expiry of the truce in 1621.

However, during the following twenty years, the papal throne was occupied by a man of a very different calibre. Urban VIII (1623–44) was above all an Italian prince interested in the technical aspects of war – he fortified Castel St. Angelo in Rome, set up a gun factory in Tivoli and transformed the Vatican library into an arsenal. Of an absolutist disposition, Urban was impatient

of the partnership of the cardinals in the affairs of the Church or
the Papal States and even more of the tutelage the Emperor and
the king of Spain. Urban therefore helped to break the Spanish
–Austrian hold over Italy in the war of the Mantuan succession
(1627); and the duchy of Urbino was incorporated in the Papal
States after the death of its last duke (1631) – both in the face
of imperial and Spanish opposition. Whether Urban actively
subsidized Gustavus Adolphus is a matter of dispute; he certainly
welcomed the successes of the Swedish and French armies. But
Urban's vain protest against the peace of Prague (1635) was a
clear indication of the impotence of the Curia in the face of the
secularization of international politics.

### Northern and Eastern Europe

Since 1569, when the Union of Lublin merged the kingdom of
Poland and the grand-duchy of Lithuania, Poland had been
the preponderant power in eastern and north-eastern Europe.
In size, population, commerce and industry, agriculture and
forestry, Poland surpassed all her neighbours. It included present-
day Poland, Lithuania, Latvia, Byelorussia, the Ukraine, East
Prussia and Danzig. The flourishing towns contained an active
population of citizens and Jews – both to a large extent the descendants of immigrants from Germany – and the numerous petty
noblemen, the 'szlachta', were adroit businessmen in trading the
products of their vast estates. Polish horsemen, especially the
cossacks of Volhynia and Podolia, trained in a ceaseless border-
warfare against Turks and Muscovites, were the best light cavalry
to be found anywhere.

Large tracts of the country had embraced the Lutheran creed,
but the counter-reformation effected the complete return of the
nation to the Roman obedience. The counter-reformation,
however, did not affect the duchies of Prussia, Courland and
Livonia, which were fiefs of the Polish crown under their own
rulers and their own constitutions. These duchies, together with
the free city of Danzig, occupied virtually the whole seaboard and
every notable port of the kingdom. Their anomalous position
points to the main weakness of Poland's seeming pre-eminence,
namely its lack of central direction. After the extinction of the
Jagellon dynasty (1572) Poland became an elective monarchy
and the Polish crown was, until the annihilation of the country in

1795, the coveted object of international rivalry. The first elected king, the duke of Anjou, left the country after thirteen months to become Henry III of France; his successor, Stephen Bathory, voivode of Transylvania, died childless after a reign of eleven years (1586). The next king, Sigismund III, son of John of Sweden, was luckier in that his two sons were successively elected after him, so that the Vasa dynasty ruled Poland for about eighty years. But by this time the morals of the electing noblemen had been thoroughly corrupted by bribery, and their increasing influence upon the 'royal republic' was eventually made unassailable by the formal confirmation of the 'liberum veto' in 1652, by which one dissenting vote was sufficient to 'tear up' all legislative and other decisions of a diet; aristocratic anarchy was the hallmark of the Polish constitution.

The reign of Sigismund III (1587–1632) saw the peak as well as the beginning of the decline of Polish power. Skilfully exploiting the 'troubles' which afflicted the grand-duchy of Moscow after the death of the last ruler of the Rurik dynasty (1598), Sigismund supported two pretenders against the new rulers, Boris Godunov and his son Fyodor (1598–1605) and Vasilij Shuiskij (1606–10); and when either 'false Dmitri' had been slain, a Polish army invaded Moscow and the Russian boyars were forced to elect as their tsar Wladislaw, Sigismund's eldest son (1610). For two years Russia was a Polish satellite. Russian nationalism and Orthodox fanaticism expelled the foreigners in 1612, and the machinations of the prelate (later patriarch) Philaret succeeded in the election as tsar of his son Michael (1613), the ancestor of the Romanov dynasty which was to rule Russia until 1917.

Acting on the principle that my neighbour's neighbour is my friend, Shuiskij concluded the first Russo-Swedish alliance in 1609; and Philaret, until his death in January 1633 the chief adviser of his son, and Michael himself (died 1645) continued to regard Sweden as their natural ally against Poland.

In some respects Sweden's position at the beginning of the seventeenth century can be compared with that of France, and both countries therefore pursued similar policies. The encirclement of France by the Habsburg powers had its counterpart in the ring the united kingdoms of Denmark and Norway had laid round Sweden. The only open frontier Sweden possessed was along the eastern boundary of Finland, conquered and christianized by the Swedish kings in the twelfth and thirteenth centuries;

but this frontier led nowhere and therefore played no part in either offensive or defensive strategy. For the rest, Denmark–Norway owned districts that have since become fully integrated into Sweden proper: the counties of Jämtland in central Sweden, of Bohus, Halland, Malmöhus, Blekinge, Kristianstad in the south-west and south, and the island of Gotland in the Baltic sea; and in addition the Baltic islands of Oesel, since 1721 part of the Russian empire, and Bornholm. Danish possession of both shores of the Sound meant Sweden's exclusion from access to the North Sea; Danish Gotland was a permanent threat to the eastern seaports between Kalmar and Stockholm and, together with Danish Bornholm, a menace to Swedish communications with the opposite shore from Riga to Lübeck, while Danish Oesel was a ready stepping stone for any invasion of Estonia, which Sweden had acquired in 1561–82.

The desire to free Sweden from Danish pressure and thereby obtain safe access to the German and Polish shores of the Baltic, as well as the free passage out of the Baltic, had therefore been the natural aim of the Vasa kings ever since Gustavus I (1523–60) had freed Sweden from Danish political rule and Lübeck's commercial control. The Danish–Swedish rivalry for what the diplomatic language of the time called the *dominium maris Baltici* derived from political and economic considerations; religion played no part in it as both countries had adopted the Lutheran Reformation. Competition grew fierce after the virtual monopoly which the German Hanse had exercised over the north European trade for more than three centuries collapsed and Dutch and English shipping steadily increased their direct trade with the Baltic ports. What the Baltic region had to offer to the markets of Western Europe was a variety of raw materials on which the livelihood of the industrialized areas of the west and the very existence of those overpopulated countries were dependent: Norwegian cod, Swedish copper and iron, Russian hemp, tar, honey and timber, Polish and East German grain – these were the most marketable and most indispensable products of the Baltic hinterlands. Denmark was in firm possession of the entry and exit through the Sound, and for centuries the Sound dues constituted the backbone of the Danish revenue system. Control of the ports and customs sheds from Reval to Kiel, of the estuaries of the rivers from the Narva to the Schlei was the principal issue of the fight for the *dominium maris Baltici*.

In the north Estonia had become a Swedish province in 1582; in the west the duchies of Schleswig and Holstein had for centuries been appanages of the Danish crown. The prizes to be gained were therefore the intervening Polish fiefs of Livonia, Courland and Prussia, the German duchies of Pomerania and Mecklenburg, and the more or less independent Hanseatic cities of Riga, Danzig, Stralsund, Rostock, Wismar and Lübeck.

The crowns of the Nordic kingdoms were elective from early Germanic times. The actual power lay with the aristocracy, ruling through the council of state (*Riksråd*); the extent of the royal power was entirely dependent on the personal strength or weakness of the sovereign in relation to the Estates of the realm. Citizens and peasants were chafing under the aristocratic yoke as much as the king and therefore inclined to make his cause their own.

The great popularity of Christian IV of Denmark (1588–1648) – whose memory is preserved to this day in the Danish national anthem – is no doubt due largely to his vigorous promotion of the mercantile interests of the middle classes. In reality, his setting up of an East India Company (1614) to rival the English, Dutch and French companies, the foundation of Glückstadt (1616) to outstrip Hamburg as an international emporium, the establishment of a factory in Tranquebar in the Carnatic (1616) in competition with the Portuguese and Dutch – all these enterprises were doomed to failure as were his attempts to overpower Sweden in the Kalmar war (1611–13) and to make himself the master of Lower Saxony in the Danish war (1625–29). The net result of Christian IV's reign was the definite loss of Denmark's supremacy in northern affairs.

Sweden's aggressive and expansionist foreign policy began under the ambitious sons of Gustavus I, Eric XIV (1560–68) and John III (1568–92). John, who had been installed as duke of Finland, completed the conquest of Estonia so as to gain command of the entire Gulf of Finland and thus to bar Russia's way to the Baltic. For he regarded Russia as Sweden's chief enemy and his marriage to a Polish princess was designed to gain Polish support for his anti-Russian plans. Eric, on the other hand, pursued an anti-Danish policy – for which he intended to enlist England by his proposed marriage to Queen Elizabeth – which coincided with John's designs upon Estonia where the principal port, Reval, submitted to him. The ensuing war with Denmark and

Lübeck (1563–70) went badly for Sweden. The result was a rebellion of the Swedish nobility in concert with Eric's brothers, John and Charles – it ended with Eric's deposition (1568) and murder, perhaps at John's instigation (1577). John bought his election as king with large concessions to the nobility which thus emerged as the real victor from the fraternal strife. John pursued his anti-Russian policy by having his son, Sigismund, brought up in the Roman faith, and elected king of Poland (1587). His catholicizing inclination however contributed to weakening the royal power, which was now confronted by the alliance of the nobility with the strictly Lutheran clergy who were supported by the middle classes and the peasantry. This combination had at its head duke Charles of Södermanland, the youngest and most gifted of the sons of the founder of the Vasa dynasty. A short visit of the new king, Sigismund, proved that neither the re-establishment of royal power nor that of the Roman church was feasible. When Sigismund returned to Poland in 1594, the government of Sweden was taken up by the magnates of the *Riksråd* under the nominal leadership of Charles. With the support of the clergy, citizenry and especially the peasantry, Charles had himself recognized as lieutenant-general of the realm (1595), defeated a Polish invasion of Sweden, broke the resistance of the magnates by gruesome executions of Sigismund's adherents (whom Sigismund had treacherously handed over to Charles) and eventually, in 1604, assumed the title of king. Sweden's separation from Poland coincided with a favourable peace concluded with Russia (1595), followed by an alliance and military support of Moscow against the Polish invaders (1610) and accompanied by an attempt to intensify Swedish–Russian commerce *via* the sea-route to Arkhangelsk. The foundation, with Dutch advice and assistance, of Göteborg on the small strip of land under Swedish sovereignty north of the Sound, was to serve the commercial ends of trade with the White Sea and fishery in arctic waters.

However, Charles IX's reign ended in near-disaster. Paralysed by a stroke, the king had to face a successful invasion of Sweden by Christian of Denmark and a war with Russia after the breakdown of the Russian alliance of 1609. The king's successor (October 1611) was a minor, and the high aristocracy seized the opportunity. The 'royal promise', exacted from the sixteen-year-old Gustavus II Adolphus at his accession, extended the privileges of the nobility and put the supreme power into the hands of the five-man council of state. The head of the council was Axel Oxenstierna (1583–1654) who, from December 1611 when he was appointed chancellor, was Sweden's virtual ruler for the next thirty years. His sincere friendship with the king prevented a clash between crown and nobility; but the almost continuous absence abroad of Gustavus Adolphus and the long minority of his daughter Christina had the effect that the country was completely in the hands of the Oxenstierna family and their partisans. From 1617 to 1640 three of the five councillors of state were Oxenstiernas – the chancellor, the treasurer and the justiciar.

Oxenstierna's statesmanship showed itself in the peace of Knäred (1613) which terminated the Kalmar war on fairly favourable conditions despite the great Danish successes on land and sea. Even more important was the peace of Stolbova (27 February 1617) which ended the long-drawn conflict with Russia. Here the young king had won his first military experience, and Dutch financial and economic support significantly contributed to Sweden's military and diplomatic gains. Russia ceded Karelia which secured the eastern approaches of Finland, and Ingermanland which established a land-bridge between Finland and Estonia. On the other hand Russia was given back the commercial metropolis of Novgorod through which flowed the greater part of the trade with western Europe; the city had been under Swedish administration from 1611, and the economic clauses of the peace treaty secured the continuation of the ascendancy of Swedish and German traders. Gustavus Adolphus now granted further privileges to the nobility and was crowned king – he was free to embark on an active policy against Poland.

## Germany

To speak of 'Germany' as if it were the central European equivalent of France or Spain or Sweden, is a deceptive but convenient simplification. In reality, 'the German section of the Holy Roman Empire', as was its official title, consisted of the patched-up relics of the medieval Empire, in which the age-old antagonism between the Emperor and the princes, the rivalry between the privileged group of the electoral princes and the lesser princes, the quarrels between the princes and the representative Estates,

*Central Europe*

Memel

Königsberg

PRUSSIA

SWEDEN

POMERANIA

Danzig

Stettin

NBURG

Frankfurt

Berlin

Küstrin

POLAND

ONY

SILESIA

Dresden

Friedland

Glatz

Prague

BOHEMIA

Pilsen

Jankov

MORAVIA

UPPER

Passau

Vienna

LOWER

UPPER

AUSTRIA

HUNGARY

AUSTRIA

STYRIA

Graz

——— *Limit of the Holy Roman Empire*

ARINTHIA

*The Wittelsbach dominions controlled by Maximilian of Bavaria:*———

CARNIOLA

*Bavaria*

*the possessions of his brother-in-law, Wolfgang William*

*Bishoprics held by his relatives*

*Spanish possessions*

*Austrian possessions*

*Hesse – Cassel*

*Hesse – Darmstadt*

*Palatinate*

*Archbishopric of Mainz*

*Archbishopric of Magdeburg*

and other feuds had, during the sixteenth century been overlaid and exacerbated by religious divisions.

The constitution of the Empire was based on the Golden Bull of 1356, which remained in force until 1806. It was supplemented by various 'fundamental laws' of which the 'final compact' of the Augsburg Diet of 1555 was the most important. This consisted of two parts, the 'religious peace' and the 'executive regulation'. As it turned out, both these laws were unsatisfactory compromises, the one between the aims and claims of the Catholics and Lutherans (the Calvinists were expressly excluded), the other between the cen ripetal and centrifugal tendencies of the Emperor and the Estat :s. The main weakness in both cases was the omission of any m achinery for the interpretation of their many ambiguous clausc s as well as for the enforcement of these decrees. The contention arising from this source therefore forms the background of the cold and hot wars which rent Germany until the peace of Westphalia.

The chief organs of the Empire were the imperial diet, the imperial chancery, the aulic council, the imperial tribunal and the imperial circles.

The imperial diet consisted of all the independent princes and cities of the Empire. Its legislative power was, in principle, unlimited; in practice, the execution of its laws was entirely dependent on the goodwill of the individual territories. The diet did not meet at regular intervals or at a fixed place, and no provision was made for interim committees. The 'propositions' submitted by the Emperor were debated in three separate sections or 'curias' – Electors, princes and cities – and these had to reach agreement before a proposition could be proclaimed, usually in the form of a 'final compact' (*Rezess*). The question whether the decisions within each section should be unanimous or by majority was never decided – the protest against the validity of majority resolutions made at the diet of 1529 was the origin of the appellation of 'Protestants' given to the protesting Estates.

The imperial chancery was nominally controlled by the imperial chancellor, the archbishop of Mainz, the highest-ranking German prince. In reality, the office was conducted by the vice-chancellor, a nominee of the Emperor, who had his seat at the Emperor's court in Vienna. From 1620, when a separate Austrian chancery was established, the imperial chancery ceased to be of any account.

The aulic council and the imperial tribunal were the highest courts of justice. The former, sitting in Vienna, was entirely appointed by the Emperor; the latter, in Speier, was chiefly an organ of the Electors and the circles. But the decisions of either law-court could be enforced only with the co-operation of the local rulers.

The ten imperial circles were originally (1500) established as regional organizations for the carrying out of tasks which the Empire could not fulfil or which the Estates were loath to entrust to the Emperor. The 'executive regulation' of 1555 chaiged the circles with the maintenance of public peace, in addition to which the circles soon assumed the supervision of monetary and economic matters within their boundaries. Their efficiency was largely dependent on the energy and power of the presiding princes, especially of the 'colonel of the circle' who was in charge of the military and police forces.

The religious peace of 1555 was meant to freeze the position of the two churches as prevailing in that year. However, for a while, the Lutherans continued to expand throughout northern and central Germany; and soon the revived Church of Rome began to make good its losses. The 'ecclesiastical reservation' of the religious peace was their chief legal argument: it stated that a prince of the church – bishop or abbot – who turned Protestant could not avail himself of the general principle 'cuius regio eius religio' and impose his religion upon his subjects but had to renounce his ecclesiastical dignity. A second point in dispute was the question whether the free imperial cities had the 'ius reformandi'; it was affirmed by the Protestants and denied by the Catholics. As the Catholic party had the majority in the imperial diet, the aulic council and the imperial tribunal, the Protestants could defend themselves only by paralysing the entire constitution. In 1601 they refused to acknowledge the decisions of the imperial tribunal in ecclesiastical disputes, and in 1608 they walked out of the imperial diet which did not re-assemble until 1640.

In name, the Emperor was the supreme lord at the head of this crumbling feudal pyramid. In fact, his power was dependent on the resources derived from his patrimonial possessions, the qualified support of the mass of imperial knights, counts and abbots, and temporary alliances with some prince or group of princes. What tangible authority the Emperor exercised was based on the fact that the imperial dignity had, since 1438, become hereditary by prescription in the house of Habsburg. It had accumulated, through conquest, inheritance and marriages, the greatest mass of territories in southern Germany, with the Austrian possessions as the heartland and Vienna as their capital. Moreover, the connexion with Spain had allied the Austrian Habsburgs with the leading European power. Although the Viennese archdukes were only the poor relations of their Spanish cousins, family feeling and political interest aligned the policies of Madrid and Vienna in most, if not all questions touching European affairs.

In theory, the seven Electors were the confidential advisers of the Emperor whom they, and they alone, elected and crowned. In practice, they had for centuries been the chief agents in thwarting any attempt by successive Emperors to strengthen the central power. The jealous pride with which the Electors maintained the 'electoral pre-eminence' even survived the religious split. For the three ecclesiastical Electors, the archbishops of Mainz, Cologne and Trier, were now confronted by three Protestant Electors, of Saxony, the Palatinate and Brandenburg. The position of the seventh, the king of Bohemia, was in any case doubtful while this Elector was simultaneously the elected Emperor. The aversion to having one of their number raised to royal dignity contributed to the opposition of Protestant and Catholic Electors against the Elector Palatine's assumption of the Bohemian crown in 1619. In 1630 at the supreme crisis of the 'Thirty Years War' the Catholic and Protestant Electors combined against the Emperor, forced him to dismiss his generalissimo, Wallenstein, and virtually to disband the imperial army, arrogated to themselves a decisive voice in foreign affairs, and refused the confirmation of the Emperor's son as heir apparent to the crown. It was ironic that the Electors eventually, in the peace of Westphalia (1648), lost their 'pre-eminence' to the host of the lesser princes whom they had always tried to keep in a subordinate place.

Entry into the close circle of the Electors was therefore a much coveted goal of princely policy. But even without the electoral dignity, the Bavarian Wittelsbachs were already the most powerful German rulers next to the Habsburgs. The usual historical maps give a completely wrong impression. For it was not the small duchy between Danube and Alps that made the Wittelsbachs the great princes they were. At the beginning of the Lutheran Reformation the court of Munich had coolly weighed the arguments for and against joining the Reformers; rational considerations eventually kept them on the side of the Roman Church, and this calculation proved correct. The frightened Curia conceded to the Wittelsbachs all the rights over the church which the Protestant rulers usurped in their domains. Even more, the Wittelsbachs prevailed upon the Curia to accumulate upon Bavarian princes a series of bishoprics, regardless of the prescripts of Canon Law. The neighbouring sees of Freising and Regensburg conveniently rounded off the duchy, and Freising manors extended deeply into Austrian lands. The prince-bishopric of Liège split the Spanish Netherlands in half and made its Wittelsbach ruler the neighbour of the United Provinces as well as France. The bishopric of Hildesheim established the Wittelsbachs in the centre of Lower Saxony. The greatest coup was the elevation of a Bavarian prince to the archbishopric-electorate of Cologne in 1583, when Cologne was on the point of adopting the Lutheran creed. The suffragan bishopric of Münster was added two years later. From about 1580 to 1763 Cologne, Münster, Paderborn, Hildesheim and Liège were in almost permanent occupation by Wittelsbach bishops. Thus the Wittelsbachs were the most powerful rulers not only in south-east Germany, where the Upper Palatinate fell to them in 1623, but also in north-west Germany, where in 1613 the duke of Jülich-Berg allied himself by marriage to the Bavarian Wittelsbachs.

The largest and richest Electorate was Saxony, abounding in natural resources, with a flourishing agriculture and prosperous textile and mining industries. Saxony's geographical position in the heart of Europe made the Leipzig fairs the rendezvous of buyers and sellers from the ends of the known world and the centre of German book production and distribution. The Wettiners of Saxony were uncompromisingly orthodox Lutherans in religious matters and cautiously conservative in politics. The court of Dresden viewed the religious Calvinism of the Palatinate and the republican Calvinism of the Dutch, Bohemians and Swiss with undisguised hostility, and clothed its aversion to Sweden, France and Spain with the mask of German patriotism. Fear of the Thuringian branches of the house of Wettin who never forgot the transfer of the Electorate to the Dresden line, kept the Saxon Electors mostly in the Emperor's camp, though their ambition was the formation of a 'third party', preferably in conjunction with the other Electors.

The Electorate of Brandenburg was the poorest of the larger German states. Its main source of revenue was the production of grain, which was being greatly increased through the ruthless efficiency of the land-owning nobility, the *Junkers*, who were evicting or depressing into serfdom the peasantry and creating huge latifundia where they reigned as absolute lords. No contemporary observer realized that the extent of the motley Hohenzollern lands, from Memel in far-away Prussia to Cleves on the Dutch border, made it inevitable that the Hohenzollerns should try to establish land bridges between these widely scattered territories and to obtain free access to the sea for land-locked Brandenburg.

If the politics of Saxony as well as Brandenburg lacked any purposeful drive during the greater part of the first half of the seventeenth century, the fault lay mainly in the incompetence and lassitude of their rulers. John George I of Saxony (1611–56) and George William of Brandenburg (1619–40) vied with each other in sluggishness and prevarication. Both spent the greater part of their lives besotted behind their beer-mugs; both had a special gift of alienating honest advisers, and both tamely submitted to the evil counsels of men who were open to shameless bribery by foreign potentates.

Of the non-electoral principalities, potentially the strongest were the dominions of the houses of Brunswick and Hesse. But repeated partitions had severely reduced the influence of the several branches of these dynasties. Although all Guelphs called themselves 'dukes of Brunswick-Lüneburg', each was only the sovereign of a subdivision of the old duchy: Celle, Wolfenbüttel, Grubenhagen, Göttingen, Calenberg (of which Hanover became the capital in 1636). The senseless partition of the landgraviate of Hesse among the four sons of landgrave Philip (1567) condemned the two younger branches to nullity and made the two elder branches consume their best energies in fratricidal strife. This was exacerbated when Hesse-Cassel, comprising the richer half of the original country, in 1605 introduced Calvinism and fostered intellectual and economic relations with France and the Netherlands, whereas Hesse-Darmstadt remained strictly Lutheran and sided with the imperial faction.

It was with good reason that Duke William of Jülich-Cleves-

Mark-Berg-Ravensberg (1539–92) was known to his contemporaries as William the Rich. The territories which he inherited extended from the river Weser in the east to the river Meuse in the west; they bordered on the Guelph duchies, Hesse, the United Provinces and the Spanish Netherlands, and completely surrounded the archbishopric of Cologne. They included the prosperous textile industries of Bielefeld, Hagen, Herford, Elberfeld and Barmen, the powder and paper mills of Pfaffrath and Gladbach, the ceramic industry of Siegburg and, above all, the world-famous production of swords and knives centred in Solingen. Some of the busiest overland trade routes to central Germany and thence eastern Europe started in the duke's Rhine ports of Wesel, Duisburg and Düsseldorf, which handled goods from and to the Netherlands and England (where the highly prized Solingen wares went by the name of Cologne blades). However, the chequered history of the component territories made it impossible for Duke William to establish a central administration. The Estates, that is the nobles, were the effective rulers in each of the several duchies, and their power became unassailable when William was succeeded by a feeble-minded son. Moreover, the country was rent by religious cleavages: Jülich and Berg had remained faithful to Rome, Mark and Ravensberg became Lutheran, Cleves adopted Calvinism. Political and religious inclinations therefore caused the Estates to sell themselves to whichever power seemed to offer the better security for the maintenance of their rule. The death of the imbecile John William (1609) therefore stirred into action not only the presumptive heirs and some doubtful claimants but all the great powers who were interested in either maintaining or upsetting the political equilibrium in this part of central Europe.

## Britain

In the fifty years between the death of Queen Elizabeth I (1603) and the establishment of the Protectorate (1653) British foreign policy was hampered by the unwillingness of Parliament to back even a popular policy with sufficient money-grants; and the vacillation of the Stewarts between Spain, France, the Netherlands and Denmark antagonized in turn every potential friend without impressing any actual foe. The reduction of proud Elizabethan England to a second-rate power can be seen in the cold rebuff of Charles's envoys to Vienna (1636, 1642), whose intervention for the king's Palatine relations was met with contumely; in the disrespect with which in 1643–44 the senate of Hamburg treated the rival envoys of King and Parliament; and finally in the fact that it was never suggested that Britain might be invited to the peace congress in Osnabrück (1643–48).

On the other hand, numerous Englishmen, Scots and Irishmen enlisted and took commissions in the armies or served as advisers in the council chambers of every continental power. Most of the officers who learned the military profession under Maurice of Orange and Gustavus Adolphus later played leading parts in the civil war. The Scotsman, Walter Leslie, outshone them all in accumulating positions of honour and profit; he obliged the Emperor less by his undistinguished martial exploits than by the organization of Wallenstein's assassination, and died in 1667 as an imperial count, field marshal, knight of the Golden Fleece and ambassador to the Sublime Porte. During the same years English merchants, financiers and sailors laid the foundations of the empire in India and North America, in the Caribbean and in West Africa; and publicists expounded the principles on which private enterprise was to build the greatest commercial empire.

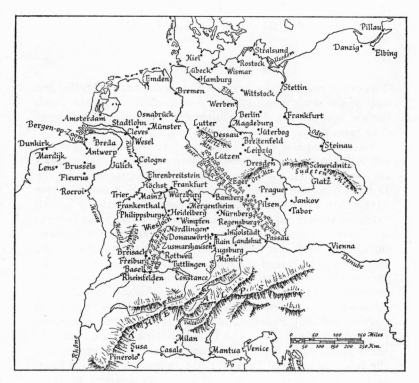

*The Topographical Background*

# CHAPTER TWO

# The European Wars 1609—60

## The Jülich–Cleves Succession

THE chain reaction of successive European conflicts in the first half of the seventeenth century was sparked off by the death without heir of Duke John William of Jülich-Cleves-Mark-Berg-Ravensberg on 25 March 1609.

The ensuing war of succession was preceded by some events which brought into the open the latent unrest of the previous decades. Molestations of the Roman Catholic minority by the Lutheran citizens of the imperial city of Donauwörth gave Maximilian I of Bavaria the desired pretext for making himself master of this city which opened the door to Swabia and brought the Palatine county of Neuburg under Bavarian control. Maximilian achieved this end by having himself nominated the executor of the ban of the empire against the recalcitrant city (1607). He seized Donauwörth and presented the Emperor with an exorbitant bill for his alleged expenses. Unable to meet these demands, the Emperor pawned the imperial city to Maximilian who immediately incorporated it into Bavaria and enforced its re-catholicization (1609). The Protestant Estates took alarm. As the imperial diet refused their demand for a re-interpretation of the religious peace of Augsburg, the Protestant members left it and, on 14 May 1608, concluded a ten-year defensive pact, the Union. It finally comprised 9 princes and 17 imperial cities, including the Electors of the Palatinate and Brandenburg, the duke of Württemberg, the margraves of Baden-Durlach, Ansbach and Kulmbach, the landgrave of Hesse-Cassel, the counts Palatine of Neuburg and Zweibrücken and the powerful cities of Strasbourg, Nürnberg and Ulm. The Elector Palatine was the director; general of the war council was Christian of Anhalt who had secured for the Union the approval and support of Henry IV of France. Its main weakness was the rift between Lutherans and Calvinists, the latter forming the great majority of the members. A further defect was the latent antagonism between princes and cities – the ones supplying ambition and arrogance, the others money and moderation. Against the Protestant Union, Maximilian of Bavaria on 10 July 1609 formed the Catholic League. It eventually consisted of 15 archbishops and bishops, 5 abbots and the city of Aachen; the Austrian Habsburgs were expressly excluded, but Philip III of Spain promised subsidies.

The dependence of the Union and League on their respective French and Spanish protectors indicated that the confrontation of the German princes could easily escalate into a European conflict. All the more important was the position the Emperor would take up. Rudolf II (1576–1612) was of a melancholy disposition which from time to time turned into insanity; his genuine interest in the arts and sciences made his capital, Prague, a seat of culture where the astronomers Tycho de Brahe and Johannes Kepler made their epoch-making discoveries. But his glaring incapacity as a ruler drove the archdukes into open revolt as they feared the break-up of the Habsburg dominions. Under the leadership of his brother Mathias, they obliged Rudolf to cede to Mathias first Austria, Hungary and Moravia (1608) and finally also Bohemia (1611).

The problem of the Jülich succession gave Rudolf an unexpected opportunity to assert his imperial rights, to increase the power of the house of Austria, to strengthen the Catholic party and to oblige his Spanish cousins. He appointed his favourite nephew Leopold, bishop of Passau and Strasbourg, as imperial commissary who was to take possession of the disputed inheritance. The legal position was indeed far from clear. On the strength of century-old compacts Christian II, Elector of Saxony, had the best claims, but he pursued them so feebly that he was soon pushed aside by the descendants of the sisters of the late John William. These were John Sigismund, Elector of Brandenburg and son-in-law of the eldest sister, wife of Duke Albert Frederick of Prussia; and Wolfgang William, son of the Count Palatine of Neuburg and the second sister.

When Archduke Leopold seized the strong fortress of Jülich in the Emperor's name, Brandenburg and Neuburg quickly agreed on the joint occupancy of the duchy. The treaty of Dortmund (10 June 1609) was mediated by the landgrave of Hesse-Cassel and guaranteed by the Union. The prospect of seeing a Habsburg prince installed in Düsseldorf was as welcome to the Spanish government in Brussels as it was repulsive to France and the Netherlands which were driven to the side of the Protestant claimants. The allied troops, reinforced by Dutch and English contingents and commanded by Maurice of Orange, expelled the archduke and took Jülich which was placed under a Dutch garrison. It was the assassination of Henry IV (14 May 1610) and the overthrow and death of Rudolf (20 January 1612) that prevented the Jülich quarrel from bursting into a European war, as both the French regent and the new Emperor Mathias (1612–19) counselled prudence. For a while a general pacification seemed possible. The imperial cities of the Union pressed for, and achieved, the disarmament of the forces of both the Union and the League. However, the 'possessing princes' fell out. Wolfgang William secured for himself the support of the League by turning Roman Catholic and marrying the sister of Maximilian of Bavaria; John Sigismund solicited the assistance of the Palatinate, the Netherlands and England by adopting Calvinism (1613). John Sigismund was incidentally the first German prince to abstain from imposing his new religion upon his Lutheran subjects, whereas Wolfgang William became a ruthless persecutor of his former co-religionists. Under French, English, Dutch and Spanish mediation the two princes agreed in the treaty of Xanten (12 November 1614) upon a preliminary division of the country. To Brandenburg were allotted the pre-dominantly Protestant duchies of Cleves, Mark and Ravensberg, and to Neuburg the mainly Catholic Jülich and Berg. But both heirs maintained their claims to the whole and the Estates of the duchy were equally anxious to preserve its unity; the administration therefore remained in the hands of the central authorities and only the revenues of the various parts were divided. Nor were the two princes successful in getting rid of their foreign allies: the towns of Wesel, Cleves, Jülich and others were in turn stormed and occupied by Spaniards and Dutch; Jülich remained in Spanish hands until 1660, Cleves and Wesel in Dutch occupation until 1672.

Meanwhile, the 'provisional treaty' of Düsseldorf (11 May 1624) confirmed the Xanten agreement; in the end, after an attempt by Brandenburg to seize Jülich and Berg by force of arms had failed (1651), Frederick William I of Brandenburg, grandson of John Sigismund, and Philip William of Neuburg, son of Wolfgang William, on 9 September 1666 concluded the treaty of Cleves, which finally divided the duchy as envisaged in 1614.

The Jülich–Cleves dispute revealed the hardening of the frontiers between the Protestant and Catholic camps, and at the same time their dependence on foreign support, military and financial. Cardinal Khlesl, the chief adviser of the Emperor Mathias, sought to exploit the temporary weariness of the combatants to achieve a 'composition' of the religious factions and thereby also consolidate the Emperor's position as the arbiter between the parties. In 1613 he obtained the admission of Austria to the League. The result was that Maximilian withdrew in a huff from the League, which Mathias eventually dissolved (1617). Khlesl's attempt to put a more conciliatory construction upon the religious peace of Augsburg was supported by the archbishop of Mainz and the Lutheran Elector of Saxony and landgrave of Hesse-Darmstadt, but neither Union nor League were willing to compromise.

For Christian of Anhalt, the most enterprising leader among the Unionists, had immensely strengthened the Union – or so he believed – by concluding alliances with England, the Netherlands and Sweden (1613) and coming to an understanding with Venice and Savoy. However, the two members, in whose support the Union had exerted itself in 1609–10, left the Union – Neuburg in 1614, Brandenburg in 1617. And when it came to the test, the majority of the allies refused to back their nominal head, the Elector Palatine, in his gamble for the Bohemian crown. This very test, on the other hand, found the League in better shape than ever before. In 1617 Maximilian of Bavaria had formed a new League with the old members of 1609, that is to say, again excluding the Habsburgs. After the outbreak of the Bohemian revolt he took advantage of the Emperor's predicament and made him formally renounce the Austrian claim to a co-directorate (8 October 1619). As the sole and unrestricted head of the League Maximilian entered the Bohemian war.

### The Bohemian–Palatine War

The so-called Bohemian war, when seen from the Bohemian-Habsburg point of view, was the last, abortive attempt of the feudal nobility of the Habsburg crownlands to preserve and, if possible, extend their constitutional, economic and social pre-rogatives against the advancing bureaucratic centralism, political absolutism and religious uniformity, which were the aims of the Viennese government. Seen in the wider European context, it was the first, unco-ordinated attempt of those nations, in which the gentry and middle classes were fostering commercial expansion, representative institutions and intellectual and religious freedom, to overcome the forces which sought to maintain or re-establish the *status quo* in politics, economics, and religion. The protagonist of the former group was the Netherlands whereas the latter was directed by the court of Madrid. The Bohemian and the European facets, the openly proclaimed and the secretly nourished aims of the various parties, their materialist and idealistic motives, the interaction of personal ambition and objective conditions – all these factors are inextricably mixed and defy any glib explanation of what was formerly considered the beginning of the 'Thirty Years War'.

Ever since the Habsburg had in 1526 acquired the 'lands of the crown of St. Wenceslas', i.e. Bohemia, Moravia, Silesia and Lusatia, the country had been governed from Prague by a group of Catholic magnates, which from the time of Rudolf II was nicknamed *facción española*, the Spanish party. Their administration, however, was in permanent conflict with the interests of the proud and impoverished nobility, jealous of their ancient rights of electing the king and lording it over the peasantry. Nor did the court party try to arrest the economic decline of the once flourishing towns; least of all was anything done to alleviate the depressed state of the agricultural tenants and workers. All classes were united in the cherished memory of the glorious Hussite past and their independence under the native king, George Podiebrad (1452–71); and the overwhelming part of the population had adopted the Lutheran creed, mainly in the indigenous version propagated by the Bohemian (or Moravian) Brethren.

The dissensions which rent apart the Habsburg brothers and cousins from 1605 were exploited by the Bohemian nobles, to form 'confederations' of the Estates of Austria, Bohemia, Moravia, Hungary and Silesia. Mathias had to buy his recognition in Austria, Hungary and Moravia with far-reaching concessions to the magnates, noblemen and municipal corporations, which virtually transformed these countries into aristocratic republics under his nominal presidency (1608–09). In Bohemia, the only dominion now left to the Emperor Rudolf, the Estates recruited an army, set up a 30-man directorate and forced Rudolf to sign the 'letter of majesty' (9 July 1609). This document guaranteed to the nobility, knights and royal boroughs and their subjects the free exercise of religion, put the ecclesiastical administration and the University of Prague under the control of the Estates and assented to the appointment of 'defensors' to supervise and uphold these laws. The letter of majesty was further enlarged by the agreement of the same day between the Protestant and Catholic Estates and on 20 August extended to Silesia.

However, the victory of the Estates over their rulers had two flaws which contributed to the ultimate defeat of the movement. The aristocratic leaders were unable to overcome the particularism of the individual crown lands; and they were unwilling to grant the citizens and peasants a full share in the rights they had won for themselves.

The 'Spanish party', directed by the Spanish ambassador and the papal nuncio in Vienna, at once took counter-measures. Rudolf called upon the 'Passau troops', which the archduke-bishop Leopold had enlisted for his enterprise against Jülich. Leopold succeeded in occupying parts of Prague, but the Bohemian Estates, including the Catholic members, allied themselves with Mathias and forced Leopold to evacuate Bohemia. This débacle finished Rudolf. The Estates elected Mathias king (23 May 1611) and he not only confirmed the pacts of 1609 but promised further political concessions. It was, however, ominous that the Estates of Moravia, Silesia and Lusatia demanded equality of rights with Bohemia and separate governments and administrations. For the disunion of the lands soon gave Mathias an opportunity to recover a measure of independence. The Estates wished to use the general diet of all Habsburg dominions, which met in Prague in June 1615, to establish a closer organization, including a common army, and to secure even more firmly their constitutional and religious privileges. They failed in every respect. The Hungarian Estates did not appear at all, and the Austrians were offended by the Bohemians and Moravians who pressed for the complete exclusion of the German language from the diets, courts and schools. The Emperor flatly refused the political and religious demands of the Estates. Nevertheless, he cajoled them into two surprising financial concessions: they renounced for five years their right of taxation – the basis of all representative assemblies – and took over a considerable portion of the royal debts.

The hollowness of the loud protestations of the Estates became clear – at least to the inner circle in Vienna and Madrid – when in 1617 the Bohemian Estates accepted, with only two dissentient votes, the Archduke Ferdinand as their king and in 1618 the Hungarian Estates followed in respect of Hungary. Ferdinand was known as the ruthless and successful suppressor of the predominantly Protestant Estates, as well as the Protestants in general in his patrimony of Inner Austria which he had from 1596 completely subjected to absolutist rule and religious uniformity. As the Emperor Mathias and his brothers were childless, the archdukes agreed among themselves to make Ferdinand the sole heir of the Austrian possessions and to work for his election as Roman king and Emperor. The objection of Philip III of Spain, who wanted his son to succeed Mathias, was overcome by the Oñate agreement, named after the Spanish ambassador in Vienna, in which Ferdinand promised to bestow upon the Spanish crown every vacant imperial fief in Italy and to cede to Spain the Habsburg and imperial possessions in Alsace, which would bridge the gap between the Franche-Comté and the Spanish Netherlands.

Encouraged by the pliability of the Bohemian Estates in Ferdinand's 'acceptance' – though not election – as king, the government re-interpreted the 'letter of majesty' in a decisively anti-Protestant sense, as far as the royal boroughs were concerned. However, the recatholicization of the town of Braunau (Broumov) was answered by the convocation of a 'Protestant diet' in Prague (6 March 1618). When its complaints were refused and its reassembly expressly forbidden, open rebellion ensued. The Protestant nobles reassembled on 21 May and the extremists, led by Count Mathias Thurn, proposed the assassination of the seven Catholic royal governors. Actually, the rebels were content to resort to the traditional Bohemian punishment of 'defenestration'. Two of the governors and their secretary were thrown out of the window of Hradčin castle (23 May). They escaped with their lives, but the break between the Habsburg king and the Bohemian Estates had become irrevocable.

Both parties were fully conscious of the wider implications of the Bohemian rebellion. They expected support from their respective foreign partisans and took the necessary diplomatic steps to secure military as well as financial aid.

The Bohemians renewed the confederation with the Silesian

and Lusatian Estates to which in the spring and summer of 1619
the Moravian and the Upper and Lower Austrian Estates ac-
ceded. They were even more anxious to come to an understanding with the United Provinces, England, Sweden, the
Protestant Union and Savoy – in fact, to mobilize the whole
of anti-Habsburg Europe. But their hopes and expectations were
not fulfilled. The Netherlands were involved in the disputes
bordering on civil war, between the Stadholder and the regents;
and the approaching end of the truce with Spain made them look
to their own defences. It was only after the execution of Oldenbarnevelt that Maurice of Orange could persuade the States-
General to grant a monthly subsidy (finally amounting to 550,000
guilders) and permit the dispatch of some regiments of horse and
foot (finally numbering about 5000 to 6000 men); one of their
commanders was the Scottish Lieutenant-Colonel John Seton.
Duke Charles Emmanuel of Savoy sent to Bohemia a regiment
of mercenaries whom Count Ernest of Mansfeld had originally
assembled for an attack on Spanish Milan. Gustavus Adolphus
sent some guns (which never reached Prague) and entered into
abortive negotiations with Moscow with a view to a diversionary
Swedish-Russian attack on Poland. The English ambassadors in
Paris and The Hague did their best to engage their government
on the side of the Bohemians, but failed to move James I from his
imaginary position as peacemaking umpire.

These lukewarm efforts of the actual and potential allies of the
Bohemians contrast sharply with the purposeful activities of the
powers which Ferdinand rallied to his side. Ferdinand's own
resources, it is true, were negligible; but his advisers – the Spanish
ambassador and the Catholic Bohemian magnates – acted with
skill and determination. Their first step was the arrest and im-
prisonment (Ferdinand himself barely prevented the assassination) of Cardinal Khlesl who was working for a compromise with
the Estates as well as against Ferdinand's election as Mathias's
successor; Khlesl's immense private fortune served to pay the
initial expenses of the campaign. However, the Vienna war party
received their greatest aid and comfort from the bungling with
which the rebels conducted their affairs. The 30 directors sequestered the property of the Catholic church and enlisted troops.
But the confiscated lands only swelled the fortunes of the noble
purchasers who made no sacrifices for the common weal; the
financial administration was disorderly, if not dishonest; the

soldiers could not be paid and, roving and pillaging up and down the country, destroyed what goodwill the masses may have had for the new order.

The death of the Emperor Mathias (20 March 1619) and the prospect of Ferdinand's election to the imperial crown exacerbated the political dissensions among the rebel leaders. A strong minority wished to establish a republic on the Dutch or Swiss model; even the majority who favoured a monarchical solution wanted only a nominal head of state, comparable to the doge of Venice. The German princes were horrified by these republican sentiments; so were James of England and Louis XIII of France. Charles Emmanuel of Savoy and John George of Saxony withdrew their candidatures; the latter eventually went over into Ferdinand's camp. The candidate upon whom the Bohemians finally agreed was the Elector Frederick V of the Palatinate, son-in-law (since 1613) of James I and head of the Protestant Union. The Estates declared Ferdinand deposed and on 26 August 1619 elected Frederick king of Bohemia.

The Bohemians could not have made a more unfortunate choice. Frederick was a pleasure-loving nonentity; James's distrust of his ability to accomplish the venture was entirely justified. His Palatine counsellors complicated matters by abandoning the original constitutional programme of the Bohemians and representing the conflict as a religious fight for the gospel. Their propaganda convinced nobody. The thoughtless attempt of Frederick's court preachers to ram Calvinist orthodoxy down the Bohemians' throats alienated the Lutheran majority of his new subjects. Worst of all, the royal council did nothing to gain the support of the middle and lower classes. Frederick's kingship was based only on the support of the radical wing of the selfish nobility who used him as their tool for maintaining their own power, and on the meagre subsidies of men and money supplied by the United Provinces – always too little and too late.

Two days after Frederick's election as king of Bohemia, Ferdinand was unanimously elected Emperor (28 August 1619), against the protest of the Bohemian representatives who had no vote. The overthrow of Frederick's kingship, the annihilation of the power of the Estates and the suppression of Protestantism in all the Austrian crownlands were now taken in hand. The Curia and the grand-duke of Tuscany sent money; Maximilian of

Bavaria pledged the League to take the field with 30,000 men;
Philip III raised 1,600,000 Spanish guilders which were to enable
the Archduke Albert, governor of the Spanish Netherlands, to
launch an attack on the Rhenish Palatinate; John George of
Saxony undertook the subjection of Lusatia and Silesia. Under
French and English pressure, the Protestant Union declared its
neutrality (3 July 1620). The only dangerous adversary in the
rear of the imperialists was the voivode Bethlen of Transylvania.
With the permission of his overlord, the Sultan, he occupied
large tracts of Hungary, advanced upon Vienna and was elected
king by the Hungarian Estates. At the same time the Sultan
inflicted a heavy defeat upon the Poles at Jassy. But Bethlen
could be bought off (June 1620), and the Sultan was deflected
from his attack upon Poland by a victorious Persian advance into
Mesopotamia. The Poles were therefore able to send a few light
horse into Silesia in support of the Emperor.

Thus, the outcome of the campaign in the summer of 1620 was
a foregone conclusion. Maximilian's general Tilly occupied
Upper Austria and the Spanish general Spinola invaded the
Palatinate; Lusatia became an easy prey to the Saxons. Tilly
from Upper Austria and the imperial general Buquoy from
Lower Austria marched into Bohemia, outmanoeuvred Frederick's general Christian of Anhalt and won a decisive victory within
half an hour at the gates of Prague in the battle of the White
Mountain (Bílá hora) on 8 November 1620.

The collapse of the Palatine kingship was instantaneous. The
royal family, with the eleven-month old Prince Rupert, fled
headlong to Silesia and thence to the Netherlands. Not a finger
was lifted by their subjects. On the contrary, all through the
year the peasants had been in open revolt and greatly impeded
the movements of the royal army. Their offer to fight the enemy
if the lords would release them from serfdom had been rejected
with contumely by the war council; the English secretary of the
queen-electress found the attitude of the peasants understand-
able and justified. The only major military success of the rebels
had been the conquest of the town of Pilsen by Mansfeld; his
officers now surrendered the place (26 March 1621). A few isolated
Dutch and Scottish garrisons held out; Wittingau (Třeboň) under
Colonel Seton was the last to capitulate (28 October 1622).

Meanwhile Spinola's Spanish-Walloon army and the League
troops under Tilly had invaded the Rhenish Palatinate.

Mansfeld, the unscrupulous mercenary, had offered his services to Ferdinand, was rebuffed, and continued the war on his own – nominally in the interest of Frederick of the Palatinate but actually in the pay of the Netherlands. Their subsidies permitted him to take over the disbanded troops of the Protestant Union, which had dissolved itself on 12 April 1621. After some minor successes against Tilly in the Upper Palatinate and the Spaniards in the Rhenish Palatinate, Mansfeld ravaged the Rhenish bishoprics and quartered his army in Alsace which he, like Bernard of Weimar later on, wished to hold as a principality.

Dutch, English and Danish diplomacy and money raised two more armies. Duke Christian of Brunswick, Protestant administrator of the bishopric of Halberstadt, carried the war into the Westphalian and Rhenish bishoprics which were under the rule of Ferdinand of Bavaria, Maximilian's brother. Margrave George Frederick of Baden, a member of the defunct Union, equipped a small army which, together with Mansfeld's troops, defeated Tilly at Wiesloch (27 April 1622) but, after their separation, was annihilated by Tilly a week later at Wimpfen. Christian of Brunswick's attempt to invade the Palatinate was beaten off by Tilly (battle of Höchst, 20 June), but he succeeded in joining hands with Mansfeld, and the two mercenaries maintained their hold over Alsace and part of Lorraine. However, Frederick of the Palatinate, who had joined the army in April, was persuaded by his father-in-law to dismiss his generals and to return to The Hague, in the vain hope of coming to an understanding with Ferdinand. Mansfeld took service with the States-General for whom he relieved Bergen-op-Zoom and conquered East Frisia which he held until the beginning of 1624.

Christian, who had returned to north Germany, tried to join Mansfeld but suffered a crushing defeat at Tilly's hands near Stadtlohn (6 August 1623) and thereafter continued his desultory warfare in Lower Saxony. But Tilly was forbidden to follow up his victory with an attack on the Netherlands for Maximilian had no mind to serve Spanish interests which here conflicted with those of his brother of Cologne and Liège and his brother-in-law of Jülich and Berg. By this time Tilly had completed the conquest of the Palatinate: he stormed Heidelberg (16 September 1622) and on 5 November Sir Horace Vere had to surrender Mannheim. Maximilian consigned the library of Heidelberg as thank-offering to Rome where the Palatina codices still form one of the most valuable portions of the Vatican library. The Bohemian–Palatinate war had come to an end.

Ferdinand was now in a position to impose his will upon all his possessions. In Bohemia and Moravia twenty-seven leaders were executed and the goods and estates of the rebels were confiscated; more than half of the landed property changed ownership. Most of it was given away or sold at cut price to Bohemian and Austrian noblemen who had stood by the Emperor, and to German, Italian and Spanish officers. In order to obtain money with which to pay military expenses and to manipulate the reorganization of the country, a colossal financial swindle was entered upon with the connivance and participation of the Emperor. The inflation which had begun in 1619 was accelerated by a systematic debasement of the silver currency in which soon every mint in Germany participated. But, as with the dissipation of the rebel lands, the crown gained least. The exorbitant gains made by the devaluation of the coinage flowed into the pockets of skilled and unscrupulous financiers and their aristocratic backers. The two biggest profiteers were the Prague merchant-banker, Jan de Witte, a native of Antwerp, and a minor Bohemian nobleman, Albrecht von Wallenstein (Valdštejn). The former had become a trusted agent of Rudolf II and was considered so indispensable that Ferdinand let him remain as the only Calvinist in Prague; Wallenstein had attached himself to Ferdinand in 1617 and emerged from the confiscation and inflation as the greatest landowner and richest man in Bohemia.

The reduction of Bohemia to complete subjection was wound up by the 'renewed constitution' of 10 May 1627. It declared the country an hereditary Habsburg possession, abolished the rights of the nobility and the towns, placed the whole administration into the hands of royal officials, made German the official language and Catholicism the only permissible religion (with certain exceptions for Silesia obtained by Saxon intervention) and moved the central chancery from Prague to Vienna. Some 30,000 Protestant families emigrated, chiefly to Saxony and Hungary; among them was Jan Amos Komenský (Comenius), the bishop of the Moravian Brethren and founder of modern pedagogics.

Similar measures were taken against the Protestant population – nobility, citizens and farmers – of Upper Austria. They resulted in a rebellion lasting from May to November 1626 which was suppressed with unparalleled savagery by the Bavarian army of occupation under the leadership of the general of cavalry, Count Pappenheim. This intervention had resulted from the Emperor's promise to cede Upper Austria to Maximilian of Bavaria in return for his support. The archduchy had to be given in pawn to Maximilian who, as the Austrian council wryly noticed, had greatly improved his arithmetic since Donauwörth – the huge account of his expenses which he drew up, enabled him to keep and drain Upper Austria from 1620 to 1628. But Maximilian's main ambition was the acquisition of the Palatinate and the electoral dignity from his cousin Frederick. As Ferdinand had promised the Palatinate to Spain, Oñate immediately objected and the Spaniards did not evacuate the Palatinate on the left bank of the Rhine. The transfer of an Electorate was disapproved not only by the Protestant Electors of Brandenburg and Saxony but also by the Catholic Elector of Mainz. Ferdinand and Maximilian had therefore to content themselves with Maximilian's provisional investiture, without prejudice to a future settlement (21 February 1623). However, there could be no doubt that Maximilian of Bavaria and Philip of Spain were the main victors of the Bohemian-Palatine war.

### The Struggle for the Grisons

Spanish armies operating from the southern Netherlands and Milan had made four important gains along the eastern frontiers of France, which ensured the security of the overland route from Madrid to Brussels and raised the hope of the Spanish government for a successful renewal of the war against the United Provinces after the expiry of the twelve-year truce in 1621. The strong fortresses of Jülich on the lower Rhine and of Frankenthal in the Palatinate were firmly in Spanish hands; Alsace had been re-occupied by the Austrians after the departure of Mansfeld; and the confederation of the Grisons and with it the Alpine passes, the highroad from Milan to the Rhine, had also been brought under Spanish-Austrian control.

Again and again the Grisons played a decisive role in the wars of the first half of the seventeenth century, wooed or betrayed, attacked or defended in turn by Austria, Spain, Venice and France. Their situation at the crossroads of central Europe gives the history of the small and thinly populated mountain valleys a

peculiar interest. Personal ambitions and local rivalries pene-
trated and poisoned all political, economic and religious issues.
There was a Spanish-Austrian party, headed by the family of
Planta, and a French-Venetian faction, led by the family of
Salis; Chur, the Protestant capital and the seat of a Catholic
bishop, usually avoided commitment to either side in order to
protect its transit trade.

When the alliance of the Grisons with Venice, concluded in
1603, expired in 1613, Austria and Spain tried to prevent its
renewal and to bind the Grisons to the Habsburg interest. But
the embargo upon the import of grain and the suspension of all
transit traffic which the Spanish governor in Milan imposed had
the opposite effect. Threatened with famine and the loss of their
livelihood, the populace yielded to the demagogy of radical
preachers, among whom George Jenatsch soon became the leading exponent. A people's court was set up in Thusis; between
August 1618 and January 1619 it condemned some 150 adherents
of the Spanish-Catholic party to torture, death, exile and fines,
deposed the bishop of Chur, expelled the French and Venetian
envoys who had protested against the lawless proceedings, and
even promised succour to Frederick of Bohemia. The pro-
Spanish faction retaliated with the massacre of about 600 Protestants in the Valtellina (18–23 July 1620), and Austrian and
Spanish troops invaded the country. Thereupon Jenatsch, who
had resigned from the priesthood, murdered Pompejus Planta
(25 February 1621) and a number of his followers. Fresh attacks
by Spaniards and Austrians followed, accompanied by wild
excesses and judicial murders. The articles of Milan, imposed by
the Duke of Feria and Archduke Leopold (15–16 January 1622),
dismembered the Grisons confederation and placed the remnant
under military administration. A rising under Rudolf von Salis
was cruelly suppressed, and the treaty of Lindau (30 September
1622) confirmed the Milan articles. The forcible recatholicization
of the country was begun but met with very little success;
epidemics decimated the indigenous population and caused even
greater losses among the foreign garrisons. Nevertheless, the
Spanish government had full control of the vital Alpine passes.

### The Danish War

The disastrous outcome of the Bohemian war forced the United

Provinces to redouble their efforts against Spain. For the year 1621 inaugurated a new and vigorous policy in Madrid and Brussels. The end of the truce coincided with the deaths of Philip III and the Archduke Albert. This brought the southern Netherlands, nominally under the governorship of Albert's widow, under the direct control of Madrid; and the leading minister of the new king, the 'Condeduque' de Olivárez (1587–1645), resumed the aggressive policy of Philip II. The war was renewed as a joint military and commercial enterprise. Spinola, his lines of supply across the Alps and down the Rhine secure, began an offensive. It started with the capture of Jülich (February 1622) and, despite a rebuff before Bergen-op-Zoom, culminated in the spectacular surrender of the fortress of Breda (5 June 1625) immortalized in Velasquez's painting 'Las lanzas'. The new Stadholder Frederick Henry (Maurice had died on 23 April) had been unable to raise the siege. At the same time Olivárez tried to damage the Dutch shipping trade with the Iberian peninsula as well as the Baltic. In both directions the Dutch (and, to a lesser degree, the English) had, from the mid-sixteenth century, been taking the place formerly occupied by the now declining Hanse towns. Olivárez planned an 'almirantazgo', a large-scale shipping and trading concern, the partners of which should be Spain, the Spanish Netherlands, the Hanse towns and Poland. The Emperor and the Catholic League were to co-operate, the former by issuing appropriate commercial laws and ordinances, the latter by occupying suitable bases on the North Sea and Baltic coasts.

It was this combination of political and economic threats which helped the Dutch diplomats in bringing about a new coalition. The breakdown of the planned marriage of the Prince of Wales with a Spanish princess had also turned James I against Spain, while the re-entry of Richelieu into the royal council, of which he soon became the first minister, heralded a new, forceful phase of French policy. Dutch diplomats thus found little difficulty in concluding an alliance with Britain and France in June 1624. Moreover, the election of Cardinal Barberini as Pope Urban VIII (6 August 1623) reversed the attitude of the Curia which, for the next twenty years, was consistently anti-Spanish.

Searching for a general to implement their military plans, the allies oscillated between the kings of Sweden and Denmark. Gustavus Adolphus submitted a grand strategic conception which was to bring Poland and Pomerania under Swedish control and to restore Silesia, Bohemia and Moravia to Frederick. The triumphal progress of the Swedish army was to lead to Vienna where peace would be dictated. The English probably preferred from the beginning Christian of Denmark, James's brother-in-law. He, like James, had observed strict neutrality during the Bohemian war. He now wanted to get the better of his Swedish rival, and wished to annex to the Danish crown the Protestant bishoprics of Bremen, Verden, Minden, Halberstadt and to gain control, if possible possession, of the Hanse cities of Hamburg, Bremen and Lübeck. He therefore proposed to eject the imperialist and League troops from Lower Saxony and then to relieve the Spanish pressure upon the Netherlands. This plan was adopted by the convention of The Hague (9 December 1625), which bound together the Netherlands, England, Denmark and Frederick of the Palatinate, while France, prince Bethlen of Transylvania and the latter's souzerain, the Sultan of Turkey, declared their assent.

The plan of campaign envisaged a fourfold advance. Christian of Denmark was to overpower Lower Saxony; Christian of Brunswick was to attack the Wittelsbach bishoprics in Westphalia and the lower Rhineland; Ernest of Mansfeld, appointed generalissimo of the coalition, was to advance against Bohemia, Silesia and Moravia; Bethlen was to operate against Austria and Moravia and effect a conjunction with Mansfeld.

A great change had meanwhile taken place in the composition of the imperial forces. The Emperor and the Spaniards were chafing against Ferdinand's military dependence upon the League and his obligations towards Maximilian of Bavaria. Wallenstein offered his personal services and his financial and economic resources to procure for Ferdinand freedom of action. Ferdinand grasped at this opportunity. Already 'colonel of Prague', 'governor of the kingdom of Bohemia', and 'prince of the Holy Roman Empire', Wallenstein was in April 1625 appointed generalissimo ('capo') of all imperial troops. When the promised recruitment of 24,000 men succeeded beyond expectation, he was elevated to the rank of duke of Friedland (13 June 1625). Friedland was the centre of the huge landed property in north-eastern Bohemia which Wallenstein had bought up with devalued money. The duchy now became the arsenal which produced arms and munitions as well as food supplies and wearing apparel for any solvent belligerent – including the Dutch. Jan de Witte acted as Wallenstein's financial agent and had no difficulty in raising loans from German, Dutch and French creditors.

In September 1625 Wallenstein started from Eger northwards and occupied the Protestant bishoprics of Magdeburg and Halberstadt. An attempt by Mansfeld and John Ernest of Weimar who commanded a Danish contingent, to break through the imperial troops and march into Bohemia, was thwarted by Wallenstein at the crossing of the river Elbe near Dessau (25 April 1626). But Wallenstein could not prevent the enemy from reaching, on a circuitous route through neutral Brandenburg and Saxony, Silesia and Moravia where they waited for Bethlen's advance from Hungary.

Meanwhile Tilly had been favoured by the sudden death of Christian of Brunswick at the age of 25 (16 June 1626). He could therefore concentrate his forces against Christian of Denmark, who had early in 1626 occupied the whole of Lower Saxony and the Westphalian bishoprics of Münster and Osnabrück. The king's incompetence as a general countervailed the bravery of the Danish army: the defeat at Lutter (27 August) forced Christian to abandon the greater part of Lower Saxony which fell into Tilly's hands.

The promising campaign in Silesia, Moravia and Hungary eventually failed, owing to a concatenation of circumstances as well as the fault of the generals. Mansfeld, John Ernest and Bethlen could not co-ordinate their efforts. Bethlen and the Sultan were interested only in the consolidation and extension of Turkish rule in Hungary; the duke of Weimar, advised by Bohemian emigrés, wished to advance into Bohemia and thence into the Palatinate; Mansfeld pitched his hope on an agreement with Venice and wanted to make northern Italy the main theatre of war. None of the generals was willing to call upon the assistance of the people who, as the peasants' revolt in Upper Austria demonstrated, might have risen against the Habsburg yoke. Nevertheless they gladly accepted native officers and soldiers to fill the depleted Danish regiments. In the end all their plans came to nothing. Late in the year both Mansfeld and John Ernest died and Bethlen made peace with the Emperor. Some 12,000 Danes, Bohemians and Germans maintained themselves in Upper Silesia until July 1627, when Wallenstein overpowered them; only some troops of horse escaped to Pomerania.

Wallenstein then turned to Lower Saxony and, in co-operation with Tilly, ejected the Danes from the Empire and pursued them into Jutland. During this year 1627 it became clear that military and political superiority had shifted from the League to the Emperor. Wallenstein assigned Tilly a subsidiary military role in Lower Saxony and elbowed him out of Mecklenburg and Pomerania. The seizure of these duchies, above all of their ports, now became the principal object of imperial policy. The great project of October 1624, the 'almirantazgo', was to be put into effect. The moving spirit behind this enterprise, Gabriel de Roy, was appointed 'commissary general of the Atlantic and Baltic seas', with his seat in the Mecklenburg port of Wismar. Wallenstein was enfeoffed with Mecklenburg (26 January 1628), whose dukes paid dearly for their adherence to the Danish cause, and appointed 'general of the whole imperial armada as well as general of the Atlantic and Baltic seas' (21 April). On the same day, his patent of generalissimo of the land forces was extended so as to give him exclusive power for the recruitment and disbandment of all troops and the appointment and promotion of all officers up to the rank of colonel.

The ambitious economic projects of Madrid and Brussels greatly appealed to Wallenstein's fertile imagination. He quickly grasped the concept of sea power which had hitherto completely escaped him. A few months earlier, on his way from Silesia to the coast, he had naïvely believed the cargo-barges on the river Oder to be ocean-going capital ships. He now realized the possibilities which the 'almirantazgo' offered to the prospective partners. At the same time he clearly foresaw that this project required a firm hold on a number of maritime bases and the willing co-operation of the maritime powers. Collaboration with Sweden was out of the question; but the Hanse towns and Denmark might be won over. Wallenstein's duchy of Mecklenburg comprised two Hanseatic ports, Wismar and Rostock; Wismar was persuaded to accept an imperialist garrison at the end of 1627, Rostock opened its gates in October 1628. More important than either was Stralsund in Pomerania, and Wallenstein's field marshal von Arnim laid siege to it. A Danish landing on the Pomeranian coast was beaten off, but, with no ships to patrol the seaward approaches, Wallenstein was unable to prevent the provisioning of Stralsund by both Denmark and Sweden. The siege had to be raised (August 1628).

In order to draw Denmark into the Habsburg orbit, Wallenstein prevailed upon the Emperor to grant Christian very lenient
conditions. The peace of Lübeck (22 May 1629) restored to him
all his possessions and only obliged him to withdraw from further
interference in the affairs of the Empire. Moreover, Christian
was given an economic bonus. The Spanish agent de Roy moved
his headquarters to Glückstadt, Christian's recent foundation on
the mouth of the Elbe. A treaty with Spain (October 1630)
envisaged Glückstadt as the staple on which should be centred the
whole Spanish trade with the hinterlands of the North and Baltic
seas. The build-up of an imperial navy had made such good
progress that it worsted the Swedish fleet in an engagement off
Wismar. Shutting out any German navy from the open sea was
therefore one of the secret war aims discussed by the Swedish
council of state a few weeks afterwards (October 1629).

The defection of Denmark from the Hague alliance was
followed by that of England – which had been in arrears with
the promised subsidies and had endangered the coalition by
Buckingham's senseless expedition against France. But it was the
Swedish successes in Poland, French strategic gains in Italy, and
the revolt of the German Electors that nullified the victory over
Denmark and buried the political and economic schemes of
Habsburg dominion.

### The Swedish-Polish War

The policy of Gustavus II Adolphus, his chancellor Oxenstierna
and the ruling aristocratic coterie aimed at making Sweden the
paramount power in northern Europe. The citizens and peasants
were however in sympathy with these aggressive designs. The
economic basis of Swedish power was the export of high-grade
iron and copper. Their main market was Amsterdam, and
Dutch advisers played a leading role in guiding Swedish finances
and trade. In order to supplement the profits from exports of
these indigenous raw-materials, the acquisition of the eastern and
southern Baltic ports was the immediate objective, for through
their custom houses passed the shipments of eastern-European
grain, timber, tar, hemp and other commodities without which
the industrial west could not exist.

The peace of Stolbova (1617) cut off Russia from the Baltic
and thus brought Russia's foreign trade under Swedish control,
except for the arduous route via Arkhangelsk.

The Polish ports were the next target. It was the more attractive to Gustavus as it opened the prospect of supplanting his cousin Sigismund on the Polish throne; but this notion was vetoed by the Swedish council of state. In 1621 the Swedish army invaded Livonia. Riga, which controlled the mouth of the river Dvina and with it the Lithuanian hinterland, fell in September. The extensive Livonian estates were parcelled out among the Swedish officers. Gustavus then moved on into Prussia (1626) and campaigned victoriously against the Poles and their vassal, the Elector-duke of Brandenburg-Prussia. By 1629 the Prussian ports of Memel, Pillau and Elbing were in Swedish hands; Danzig bought its neutrality by entering the Swedish system – to the great advantage of its commerce with the Netherlands and England.

The peace of Lübeck was the final incentive to make the Dutch and French look to Sweden instead of Denmark as an ally for the continuation of their struggle against the Habsburg powers. With this end in view, the French mediated the truce of Altmark (25 September 1629). Poland ceded to Sweden the possession of Livonia and the administration of the Prussian customs; the latter yielding more than the whole Swedish inland revenue. Poland, like Russia, was effectively barred from access to the sea. Gustavus Adolphus was then free to intervene in Germany.

## The War of the Mantuan Succession

At the same time as the Habsburg plans were threatened in northern Europe, their position in Italy suffered a serious setback. On 26 December 1627 the last male Gonzaga died, and, according to feudal law, the imperial fiefs of Mantua and Montferrat reverted to the Empire. Ferdinand had promised the Italian fiefs to Spain and therefore disregarded the claims of the next heir, the French duke Charles of Nevers-Gonzaga. Charles established himself in Mantua, but Spain in league with Savoy occupied Montferrat. For the instalment of a French vassal in the marquisate would lay open to French arms the roads to both Turin and Milan.

Wallenstein regarded the Emperor's yielding to Spanish pressure as a grave mistake. For he foresaw that this policy would inevitably lead to active French intervention, first in Italy and thereafter elsewhere. In fact Richelieu at once took countermeasures. French troops conquered the fortresses of Susa in

Savoy and Casale in Montferrat and forced the duke of Savoy
to enter an alliance with France, Venice and the duke of Nevers.
At the same time Venetian diplomats mediated between France
and England at the peace of Susa (14 April 1629); it terminated
English intervention in favour of the Huguenots, whom Richelieu
pacified shortly afterwards by the treaty of Alais (26 June).

In the field, however, the Spanish veterans proved superior to
the raw and inexperienced French troops. The imperial troops
re-occupied the Grisons, through which they marched against
Mantua. Gallas besieged and stormed the town (18 July 1630).
Casale escaped a similar fate only through the death of Spinola
who was investing it.

Richelieu therefore turned to diplomatic pressure upon the
Emperor. His envoy dominated the meeting of the Electors at
Regensburg. The appearance on German soil of Gustavus
Adolphus left the Emperor no choice but to sign the harsh peace
of Cherasco (19 June 1631). Nevers received Mantua and Montferrat, and the imperial troops had to evacuate the Grisons which
was at once occupied by a French army under the Huguenot
duke of Rohan. Richelieu ceded part of Montferrat to Savoy
in exchange for the frontier fortress of Pinerolo which gave France
access to the plains of northern Italy. A further blow was dealt
to Habsburg rule in Italy. Pope Urban VIII used the Emperor's
predicament to annex the duchy of Urbino on the death of the
last male Rovere prince, in the face of Ferdinand's claims as
liege-lord.

### The Edict of Restitution and the Revolt of the Electors

The triumphant termination of the Danish war elevated the
Emperor to a height of power as eminent as that of Charles V
after the destruction of the League of Schmalkalden in 1547.
Ferdinand meant to make the most of it.

On 6 March 1629 Ferdinand issued the 'edict of restitution'
in the form of an imperial decree 'concerning certain grievances
of the Empire'. The edict decreed the restitution to the Roman
church of all property which Protestant princes or cities had
sequestered since 1552. Catholic prelates were re-introduced in
two archbishoprics, Bremen and Magdeburg, twelve bishoprics
and innumerable abbeys and monasteries including those which
Württemberg had secularized as early as 1534. The Catholic

Estates were authorized to expel their dissenting subjects. The Calvinists were again excluded from the benefits of the religious peace of Augsburg. The imperial commissaries who were charged with the execution of the edict were empowered to use force of arms if necessary.

To all outward appearances the edict passed itself off as a religious charter signifying the victory of the Roman Catholic counter-reformation and was therefore certain of the approval of every Catholic Estate of the Empire. But the possession of the ecclesiastical principalities was at least as much a matter of political power and financial revenue as of religious confession. It is significant that the archbishopric of Bremen and the bishopric of Halberstadt were bestowed upon Ferdinand's son, Leopold William, and that Francis William of Wartenberg, an illegitimate Wittelsbach, received the bishoprics of Minden and Verden in addition to his see of Osnabrück. The edict of restitution in fact established Habsburg-Wittelsbach rule over north-west Germany. It is moreover, primarily, a constitutional document. Couched in the terminology of the religious conflicts of the preceding century, the edict established in unmistakable terms the imperial prerogative to interpret and revise the acts of the imperial diet without consulting the legislative. The edict thus consigned to the Emperor those very dictatorial powers which the princes of the empire, above all the Electors, had for centuries been concerned to restrict. In the resistance to Ferdinand's absolutist schemes, Electors, princes and cities, Catholics, Lutherans and Calvinists found common ground and readily combined for common action.

The resentment of the princes was further intensified by the high-handed treatment threatened or meted out to members of their class. While the elevation to the electoral dignity of Maximilian of Bavaria still rankled, a simple imperial fiat was again considered sufficient to deprive the dukes of Calenberg, Wolfenbüttel and Mecklenburg of their lands. They had been active adherents of Denmark; their punishment was to reward the imperial generalissimo and the generals of the League. But Tilly prudently preferred a donative of 400,000 guilders to the duchy of Calenberg; and Pappenheim's desire to become duke of Wolfenbüttel was thwarted by Maximilian – the general had to be content with the title of an imperial count. Wallenstein, on the other hand, received the duchy of Mecklenburg as an hereditary imperial fief, which put him on equal footing with the ancient dynasties. With his usual energy Wallenstein looked after the finances and economics of the duchy, which enjoyed an unaccustomed prosperity under his rule.

The unexampled increase of power of the Emperor was conditional upon the military and financial resources which Wallenstein had put at Ferdinand's disposal. The opponents of imperial predominance therefore directed their efforts towards undermining Wallenstein's position. This stratagem allowed them to pose as faithful lieges who only wanted to protect the Emperor against the presumptions of an overmighty subject. Wallenstein's novel methods of logistics provided his adversaries with plausible arguments. He acted on the principle that the districts which his army protected, as well as those which his army conquered, should supply or supplement the money and provisions necessary for the maintenance and satisfaction of his troops. Billets were therefore imposed and contributions levied in Catholic as well as Protestant territories, whether allied or neutral or hostile. It was at a meeting of the princes of the Catholic League in Würzburg (February 1627) that complaints against Wallenstein were first voiced. The general's employment of numerous Protestant officers and Bohemian nobles was an additional source of discontent. A meeting of the Electors of both religious groups held at Mühlhausen went considerably further. They dispatched sharp notes to the Emperor as well as to Wallenstein, in which they intimated that they would take the matter into their own hands if no redress was forthcoming (November 1627).

The crisis came at the meeting of the Emperor with the Electors in Regensburg in June–August 1630. It was summoned by the archbishop of Mainz and the Emperor felt obliged to attend, especially as he wished to use it for the furtherance of two designs of his own. He wanted to obtain the support of the Empire for the Spanish war against the Netherlands, and to secure the election of his eldest son, Ferdinand of Hungary, as king of the Romans, i.e. heir apparent to the imperial crown. The Emperor's influential father confessor, Father Lamormain, prejudiced Ferdinand against Wallenstein whose sacrifice he correctly diagnosed as the main condition of the Electors' assent to the election of the young archduke. But the actual decision was accomplished by the intrigues of Father Joseph, Richelieu's confidential agent. The *éminence grise*, as he was nicknamed by his adversaries, was officially a member but actually the leader of the French delegation whose attendance in Regensburg was ostensibly concerned with the settlement of the Mantuan succession. Father Joseph found Maximilian especially responsive to his overtures and laid the foundation of that partiality for France which determined Bavarian policy until 1813. After many weeks of haggling, Ferdinand was forced to yield to the peremptory demands of the Electors who left little doubt that they would otherwise cast in their lot with France (August 1630). Wallenstein was dismissed; the imperial army was put under the command of Tilly; the edict of restitution was to be subjected to scrutiny by the imperial diet. In return for the complete abandonment of the plenitude of power which the edict of restitution had given and Wallenstein's army had guaranteed him, Ferdinand received – nothing. The Electors flatly declined the supply of either men or money against the Netherlands or France and refused the younger Ferdinand's election.

Two months before the Emperor thus had been compelled to divest himself of his supreme authority and to deprive himself of the means of regaining it, the king of Sweden had landed in Germany.

### The Swedish War

For about two years the Swedish council of state carefully weighed and prepared the intervention in Germany. The administration of justice and taxation was reorganized, mainly on Dutch models. The finances were balanced, not least thanks to the revenue flowing in from the Livonian and Prussian ports. The army was reorganized on the basis of virtually universal conscription. The regimental units were composed of fellow-provincials, and their coherence had been further strengthened by the *esprit de corps* gained in the Polish campaigns. During these campaigns Gustavus had perfected various tactical innovations which Maurice of Orange had conceived; they amounted to the breaking up of the traditional rigid battle-array into smaller, mobile units and to the methodical co-operation of infantry, cavalry and artillery. The iron-foundries established by Dutch enterprise ensured the equipment of the army with Swedish guns and weapons. The 20,000 Swedes and Finns whom Gustavus Adolphus led to Germany constituted Europe's first national army.

The diplomatic preparation was equally careful. A confidential agent, John Adler Salvius, was dispatched to various north German courts and cities. He was instructed to emphasize the danger of the Emperor's autocratic policy to the constitutional liberties of the German Estates; the Swedish king was to be represented as the saviour of the German Estates who were too weak to save themselves. This line of propaganda Adler Salvius elaborated in two manifestos issued in five languages the day before and the day after Gustavus's landing.

The actual war-aims, which the council of state had discussed in secret sessions, were somewhat different. The final goal was the closure of all German ports and the exclusion from the high seas of any German navy 'for forty years'. The advantage and security of Sweden (*utilitas et securitas patriae*) and the conquest of Germany (*occupatio Germaniae*) were terms sufficiently elastic to be interpreted according to the successes of Swedish arms. The king was expressly admonished not to speak of a war of religion in the Protestant interest because 'the king of France would take umbrage'.

On 6 July 1630 the Swedes landed on the Pomeranian island of Usedom. A fortnight later the capital, Stettin, was entered and the duke had to sign a treaty of alliance. This opened to Sweden all Pomeranian towns, above all the port of Stralsund, and thereby secured a firm military and administrative base on German soil. In addition the duke had to contribute 200,000 talers to the Swedish war-chest. The dukes of Mecklenburg, of course, rallied at once to the Swedish colours. Of greater importance was the adherence of two other princes. Christian William of Brandenburg, the Protestant administrator of the archbishopric of Magdeburg, hoped to regain with Swedish help the office of which he had been deprived by the edict of restitution. The city of Magdeburg was the key fortress which dominated the line of the river Elbe and laid open the roads into Lower Saxony and Thuringia; it was at once placed under a Swedish governor. Even wider prospects opened up by the alliance concluded with landgrave William V of Hesse-Cassel; it promised a foothold in central Germany with ready access to Westphalia and the Rhine and Main valleys.

However, Gustavus and Oxenstierna had their greatest diplomatic triumph in not only signing the treaty of Bärwalde with the envoys of Richelieu (23 January 1631) but in obtaining their grudging acquiescence in its immediate publication. The treaty proclaimed as its purpose the freedom of the North and Baltic seas, the protection of the commercial interests of France and Sweden, and the liberation of the German Estates from imperial oppression. Gustavus was to put into the field 30,000 foot and 6,000 horse for whose maintenance France was to pay an annual subsidy of 400,000 talers, payable in two instalments at Amsterdam or Paris. Catholic worship was not to be interfered with, and Bavaria was to be treated as a French associate. Neither partner was to conclude a separate peace during the five-year period of the treaty's validity. The publication of the treaty compromised the French cardinal as an open ally of the Protestant power and made it difficult for him to go back on his undertakings. On the other hand, there was no clause which effectively limited Gustavus's freedom of action.

The main obstacle in Gustavus's way actually came from the two powers which he considered his natural allies and whose co-operation was indeed indispensable at this juncture: Saxony and Brandenburg. Both Electors wanted to preserve the neutrality of their countries; unlike the francophile Maximilian of Bavaria, they objected to all foreign entanglements. John George of Saxony therefore convened a meeting of Protestant princes and cities at Leipzig (February–April 1631). It was well attended but addressed only a paper remonstrance to Ferdinand. This took up the complaints of the Regensburg meeting of the Electors and added the edict of restitution to their grievances. Ferdinand returned a dusty answer. He would not revoke the edict of restitution and sternly forbade any assistance to the king of Sweden.

Gustavus could not afford to waste precious time. Brandenburg was his first goal. He quickly ejected the imperial troops from the Neumark, took Frankfurt by storm and secured the Oder line to guard his rear against Poland and to open the door into Silesia. The Elector George William, although the brother-in-law of both Frederick of the Palatinate and Gustavus Adolphus, still hesitated to accede to Gustavus's demand. George William's deliberate protraction of the negotiations, and the refusal of John George to open the fortress of Wittenberg on the Elbe to the Swedes, made possible the conquest of Magdeburg by Tilly. Gustavus, keenly aware of the loss of prestige, now pointed his guns upon Berlin; at last the Elector's resistance collapsed. Only Küstrin was allowed to keep a Brandenburg garrison; the rest of the

Electorate was occupied by the Swedes who were to receive a monthly maintenance of 30,000 talers.

The position of the combined League and imperialist troops, now under Tilly's sole command, was rather precarious, although they had been reinforced by the contingents released from the Mantuan war. Wallenstein's best general, von Arnim, had exchanged the imperial service for that of Saxony; he was now building up a Saxon army which was to back John George's policy. Tilly had made his winter quarters in Mecklenburg and northern Brandenburg. The condition of his troops was deplorable. They were dependent for food and arms on the supply, down the rivers Oder and Elbe, from Wallenstein's Bohemian and Silesian magazines. But Wallenstein made his co-operation dependent on cash payment at prices fixed by himself; and the administrators of his duchy of Mecklenburg were directed to meet Tilly's demands with indifference.

When an imperialist raid into Pomerania was repelled and the Swedish conquest of the Neumark had interrupted Tilly's communications with Poland and Silesia, the situation became intolerable. Tilly's second-in-command, Pappenheim, suggested that advantage should be taken of the preoccupation of the Swedes in Brandenburg to attack the wealthy city of Magdeburg, which could then be exploited as the pivot of future operations. After a siege lasting over a month, the city was stormed on 10/20 May. As all previous summonses to surrender had been rejected, the town was handed over to the soldiery to be sacked – in accordance with contemporary law and custom. The murder of thousands of men, women and children, and the wanton destruction of property and provisions by the enraged and starving conquerors were overshadowed by an unforeseen catastrophe. Fires broke out here and there; attempts to put them out, undertaken by Tilly and such officers as were sober and willing, were fruitless. Within a few days the whole of the town, except the cathedral and a few churches, was burnt to the ground. Magdeburg was lost as soon as it was gained.

The responsibility for the conflagration has been hotly disputed (like that of Moscow in 1812). It seems certain that Pappenheim set on fire two houses in the vain expectation that the citizens would cease fighting in order to extinguish the flames. However, his own troops, who were completely out of hand, took this as a licence to add arson to pillage. The one man who was undoubtedly guiltless was Tilly: to him, the destruction of Magdeburg meant

the ruin of his whole plan of campaign. But it was on Tilly that
Swedish and French propaganda at once fastened the blame. It
was a godsent opportunity to gloss over Gustavus's failure to
relieve Magdeburg and to blacken further the reputation of the
imperial army – did not the sack of Magdeburg substantiate the
complaints against its oppressive and licentious behaviour which
the German princes themselves had voiced?

Adler Salvius continued his activities among the Protestant
Estates, and ambitious princes began to offer their services to the
king of Sweden. Among them were three brothers of the house
of Saxe–Weimar, whom their uncle, John George, had cheated of
part of their inheritance during their minority; the youngest,
Bernard (born in 1604), was to become the most outstanding
military leader after Gustavus's death. The dukes of Mecklenburg
reoccupied their duchy. Brandenburg had been forced into
compliance. Saxony at last joined the Swedish side as the result
of a serious miscalculation of Tilly's.

Owing to his double role as general of the League and the
imperialist army, Tilly found himself torn between the contra-
dictory commands of his two masters. Maximilian of Bavaria had
just signed a treaty with France (8 May) which, in accordance
with the treaty of Bärwalde, put him and his lands under French
protection. In return for France's recognition of his title to the
Palatine Electorate, Maximilian promised benevolent neutrality
to France and France's allies. He therefore warned Tilly to
refrain from hostile actions against the Swedes and their allies.
On the other hand, Tilly considered it his duty to hold Saxony
on the Emperor's side. Tilly thought he could achieve this by
terror and force. He invaded Saxony at the end of August and
stormed Merseburg and Leipzig, which supplied him with the
booty and the strongholds that had escaped him at Magdeburg.
The result was, however, that John George at last accepted the
Swedish alliance and put his army at Gustavus's disposal (11
September).

The combined Swedish and Saxon forces met the imperialist
and League troops at Breitenfeld, a few miles north of Leipzig
(17 September 1631). Gustavus's new tactics proved superior
to the classical Spanish battle-order. The raw Saxon levies under
Arnim, it is true, fell an easy prey to the imperialist onslaught;
and John George was the first to flee headlong from the battlefield. But the Swedish infantry under Banér and Horn withstood

Pappenheim's seven cavalry charges; the Swedish guns directed by Torstenson smashed Tilly's massed squares, and the Swedish horse under Gustavus Adolphus completed the rout of the imperialists. Tilly lost 7,000 dead, an equal number of prisoners and, after the battle, 5,000 deserters of his original 36,000 men, as well as his whole artillery and the war-chest of the League. The Swedish casualties amounted to 1,500 out of 26,000, not counting the Saxons.

Both victors and vanquished divided their forces after the battle. Pappenheim covered the first stages of Tilly's retreat and then took up a position in the Weser region, pursued by Swedish detachments with whom the Guelph dukes now openly co-operated. Tilly fell back southwards, finally to Ingolstadt, the fortress on the Danube guarding the northern frontier of Bavaria. Gustavus contrived to commit John George openly against the Emperor. The Saxon army was detailed to march into Silesia and Bohemia, and on 15 November Arnim occupied Prague which Wallenstein had evacuated without any show of resistance.

Gustavus himself triumphantly advanced into the heart of Germany. By Christmas, the whole of Thuringia and Franconia had been occupied by the Swedes; a detachment under Bernard of Weimar had even taken Mannheim in the Palatinate. Gustavus made Mainz his winter quarters, surrounded by dozens of German princes and representatives of the imperial cities. The archbishop of Mainz and the bishops of Würzburg and Bamberg had fled their territories. In order to escape a similar fate, the archbishops of Trier and Cologne threw themselves on the mercy of France. The Trier fortresses of Ehrenbreitstein and Philipps-burg received French garrisons; the Moselle and the lower Rhine regions were therefore beyond Gustavus's grasp. All the other conquered territories were placed under Swedish administration of which Oxenstierna was appointed governor-general with head-quarters in Frankfurt. The bishoprics of Bamberg and Würzburg were bestowed upon Bernard of Weimar as a Swedish fief under the name of the Duchy of Franconia.

The fact that Gustavus's career was cut short after only a few more months, makes it impossible to obtain a clear picture of his ultimate aims. Most likely, he had no fixed plans but skilfully and realistically adapted them to the changing conditions. Gustavus probably only toyed with the idea of having himself elected Emperor. He seems to have planned the formation of a *corpus bellicum et politicum*, a Swedish protectorate over the greater part of Germany, as a more feasible project. His demands were certainly increasing. The pretence of alliances between equals no longer veiled the 'directorium absolutum' which the king now imposed upon the newcomers, such as the rulers of Hesse–Darmstadt, Württemberg, Ansbach, Bayreuth, Lauenburg and Solms. Frederick of the Palatinate, who joined Gustavus early in 1632, was made to understand that he would regain his lands only as a vassal of the Swedish crown. Richelieu's envoys fared no better; apart from securing protection for Trier and Cologne, they had to accept Gustavus's own interpretation of the treaty of Bärwalde. However, France obtained an immediate advantage from the Swedish presence in Mainz and Mannheim. The duke of Lorraine, a zealous member of the Catholic League and a declared partisan of Spain, was powerless to resist a French attack and had to admit French garrisons in his capital, Nancy, and several fortresses.

Gustavus resumed military operations in March 1632. Through Nürnberg he marched against Tilly's position at Ingolstadt. If the king had needed a pretext for invading Bavaria, Maximilian provided it. Disappointed by Richelieu's seeming unwillingness to rescue him – due, in fact, to Richelieu's incapacity to prevail against Gustavus's armed diplomacy – Maximilian turned to the Emperor and even asked him to reinstate Wallenstein as commander-in-chief. He himself joined Tilly's army and thereby abandoned any pretence at neutrality. Threatened by encirclement, Tilly had to fall back across the Danube to the fortress of Rain. On bridges built behind a smoke-screen and through fords covered by a massive artillery barrage, the Swedes crossed the river (15 April). Tilly was mortally wounded and died ten days later. Bavaria lay open to Gustavus. He entered Augsburg and then, accompanied by Frederick of the Palatinate, the capital Munich, which had to ransom itself with 200,000 talers.

It seemed that nothing would now prevent Gustavus from marching upon Vienna. In fact, he received encouraging messages from spokesmen of the Austrian peasants who promised to support the Swedish advance with a general rising of peasants, miners and artisans in town and countryside. Gustavus eventually decided against the invasion of Austria. For he now saw himself confronted by a new imperial army which threatened to cut his rear communications: its commander was Wallenstein.

As soon as Gustavus had landed in Germany, Bohemian emigrés established contact between Wallenstein and the king of Sweden. For these negotiations we are dependent largely on the later memoranda of the middlemen who survived Wallenstein's catastrophe by selling themselves to the court of Vienna. They ascribed to Wallenstein their own wishes and dreams which were as chimerical as those of emigrés at all times and places. In fact, Wallenstein had not changed the low opinion of his Bohemian compeers which had kept him away from the Bohemian rebellion. Nor did Gustavus trust them; least of all he trusted Wallenstein's real or alleged offers. Wallenstein's demand that a considerable portion of the royal army should be placed under his command, was flatly refused; three regiments was the most Gustavus would let him have. The future status of the Bohemian crown was deferred; Gustavus wished to settle this question in the wider context of the dismemberment of the Habsburg lands. The king was particularly worried by Wallenstein's simultaneous secret dealings with Arnim. The Saxon general allowed Wallenstein to re-occupy Prague (25 May) and a fortnight later completely evacuated Bohemia. For by this time Wallenstein had reverted to his old allegiance. The Emperor was in a desperate position. The invasion of Austria was imminent; the Catholic League was destroyed – with Bavaria, Mainz, Würzburg and Bamberg in Swedish hands, Lorraine occupied by the French, Trier and Cologne in French vassalage. But it was not only Maximilian who urged Ferdinand to recall Wallenstein but also his Polish and Spanish relations. Swedish-Russian co-operation was leading up to the war of Smolensk (see below). The Spanish treasure fleet had been captured off Cuba by the Dutch who were also making headway in Brazil; the strong fortresses of s'Hertogenbosch, Wesel and Maastricht were taken by Frederick Henry; the future prospects of economic gains in the northern waters were outweighed by the immediate danger to the southern Netherlands.

Thus pressed hard from all sides, including Wallenstein's friends at court, the Emperor had no choice but to accept the duke's conditions. At first, Wallenstein engaged himself to raise 40,000 men but refused to take over their command. However, it was his name, his financial power and his organizing genius which lured officers and men into the service, and it was clearly impossible to maintain and employ the army under any other commander. The only alternative was the king of Hungary,

Ferdinand (III); his inexperience might be compensated for by the glamour of his position as the heir apparent. But Ferdinand was expressly excluded from any command-post by Wallenstein to whom he should have been attached 'in order to learn the profession of arms'. With pretended reluctance, Wallenstein eventually (16 April) accepted the high command and shortly afterwards raised the armed strength to 70,000 men. His conditions were these; the Silesian duchy of Glogau as pawn for Mecklenburg, the enfeoffment with all territories to be confiscated and the cession of their revenues, a donative of 400,000 guilders, unrestricted authority in military matters, and full power for peace negotiations with Saxony. The only limitations concerned the troops of the League and the Spaniards, whom he could requisition only with the permission of Maximilian and the Emperor respectively; and the dealings with Saxony were to be submitted to imperial approbation. In truth, Wallenstein's position was that of a co-Emperor rather than of a subordinate.

What Wallenstein meant to do with this unparalleled plenitude of power, what ultimate aims he pursued, must remain a matter of conjecture. He has been credited with far-flung ideas such as the complete reshaping of the empire in which the Emperor (and he himself) would wield absolute power and from which all foreigners – Swedes, French, Spaniards – would be excluded. The plan has been ascribed to him of a latter-day crusade against the Turks, which would have brought the Balkans under Habsburg dominion and replaced the crescent by the cross over the Hagia Sophia in Constantinople. He has been represented as an advocate of religious toleration, as a champion of Czech nationalism, as a precursor of modern economic ideas in industry and trade, mining and agriculture. He has been condemned as a traitor and praised as a realistic statesman; he has been pictured as the victim of the unscrupulous machinations of wily courtiers and as the martyr of his honest attempts to restore peace and order in the Empire. It would seem however, that from the beginning to the end, Wallenstein was above everything else a *condottiere* in the fifteenth-and sixteenth-century tradition; and this type had by this time become entirely anachronistic. His plan, if he really had it, of transforming the German empire with the help of a mercenary army was no more feasible than the concept of Cesare Borgia, a century earlier, to remodel Italy with his hired bands. Wallenstein perished because the modern absolutist state had no room for a politico-military adventurer, whose only constant and ascertainable motive was self-aggrandisement.

After Wallenstein had thrown the Saxons out of Bohemia, he led his army into the Upper Palatinate and thereby interrupted Gustavus's lines of communication with central and northern Germany. Wallenstein effected a sham reconciliation with Maximilian who had to relinquish the command of the Bavarian troops to the imperial general. Gustavus retreated to Nürnberg. All through the summer the opponents faced each other in heavily fortified camps, both armies suffering from epidemics and lack of provisions more than from operational losses. A final desperate attempt to dislodge Wallenstein failed (3 September) and a fortnight later the armies separated. Gustavus turned again southward into Bavaria, Wallenstein marched northwards into Thuringia and Saxony. Leipzig fell to the imperialists and Wallenstein intended to rest his army in Saxon winter-quarters. But the urgent appeals of the Elector recalled Gustavus who could not afford to lose Saxony. Wallenstein's war council did not believe that the Swedes would undertake any action at this time of the year, in mid-November. Pappenheim was therefore dispatched towards the Rhine to protect Cologne against the Dutch. However, Gustavus was rapidly approaching Leipzig. Wallenstein took up a defensive position in front of the city near Lützen and hastily recalled Pappenheim. On 16 November 1632 the Swedes attacked, but the battle repeated the deadlock of Nürnberg. At nightfall, both contestants were totally exhausted, but as Wallenstein immediately evacuated Saxony and took up his quarters in Prague, the Swedes regarded themselves as victors. But their victory was bought at a terrible price. Heading one of the many cavalry charges, Gustavus was killed by three musket shots. As far as one man can influence the course of history, the death of Gustavus marked a turning point in the history of Europe – it removed the main obstacle in the way of the ascendancy of Richelieu's France.

The battle of Lützen also brought to the fore the military genius of two generals. Wallenstein's reliance mainly on defensive tactics had once again served him well, but his hasty retreat after the battle damaged his reputation as a strategist with friends and foes. The man who saved the day for the imperialist cause was Ottavio Piccolomini, a 32-year old Italian nobleman, who from the age of sixteen had fought for the Spanish and Austrian

Habsburgs and attached himself to Wallenstein's fast-rising star. The death of Pappenheim, who was mortally wounded as soon as he appeared on the battlefield of Lützen, removed his most spectacular rival for the generalissimo's favour whom he was eventually to betray and supersede. The hero on the Swedish side was duke Bernard of Weimar. When the king's death threatened to throw the Swedes into disarray, Bernard rallied them with the cry of vengeance; he captured Wallenstein's whole artillery and made the Swedish army stand their ground on the battlefield.

### Wallenstein's End and the Peace of Prague

The death of Gustavus Adolphus seemed to open the way to a general pacification. John George of Saxony considered the alliance lapsed; together with his brother-in-law, Christian of Denmark, and his son-in-law, George of Hesse–Darmstadt, he entered into negotiations with the Emperor. But this peace offensive was wrecked by the superior diplomacy of Oxenstierna. The Swedish chancellor first succeeded in keeping Brandenburg in the Swedish camp and thereby destroyed John George's hope of facing the Emperor at the head of a strong Protestant party. Thereafter Oxenstierna united the Franconian, Swabian, Upper Rhenish and Electoral Rhenish circles and Brandenburg in the alliance of Heilbronn (23 April 1633). The political directorate was assigned to Oxenstierna but the discussions at Heilbronn revealed that the chancellor did not command the firm, though reluctant, obedience the late king had imposed upon the German allies. The 'consilium formatum' of seven German and three Swedish advisers, it is true, did not greatly restrict Oxenstierna's powers of 'final resolution'; and he succeeded in inserting, for the first time, the clause of a 'Swedish satisfaction' among the terms of a future peace. But he could not persuade the Upper and Lower Saxon and Westphalian circles to join the Heilbronn confederation; and he had to agree to the restitution of the Rhenish Palatinate to the son of Frederick V (who had died a fortnight after Lützen). Oxenstierna would also have wished to appoint his son-in-law, Horn, as the allied generalissimo, but had to be content with an unsatisfactory and dangerous division of command between Horn and Bernard of Weimar. Worst of all from the Swedish point of view, Oxenstierna had to concede to

France what Gustavus had always refused, namely an active share in the supreme decisions. Richelieu's brilliant ambassador, the marquis de Feuquières, lavishly distributed gifts, pensions and loans among the German confederates, transferred the payment of the French subsidies from Sweden to the Heilbronn alliance, and achieved the parity of the two crowns: henceforth Sweden and France together were to determine any peace proposals.

The Swedish–French resolution to allow peace only on their own conditions made futile the various plans which emanated from Wallenstein, or perhaps only from Wallenstein's entourage, during the summer of 1633. He met the Saxon field-marshal Arnim, he sent a confidential agent to Oxenstierna, he was in constant contact with the Bohemian exiles; one of them, Count Thurn, was his main go-between with the Swedes; another, Count Kinsky, kept in close touch with Feuquières. He only neglected to keep Vienna informed where his enemies, led by Father Larmormain and the archduke Ferdinand, were undermining his position. In fact, Wallenstein's ideas were so nebulous and self-contradictory that he was distrusted in turn by every partner of these tortuous negotiations. In October, Arnim met Wallenstein in Silesia, fully authorized by Brandenburg and Saxony to sign a peace-treaty – when Wallenstein suddenly threw an army into Saxony. Arnim and his Saxon troops hurriedly left Silesia to protect their country, and Wallenstein forced the remaining Swedish troops to capitulate at Steinau (10 October). This success mollified the imperial court, but Wallenstein forfeited his last chance of a sincere reconciliation by his subsequent behaviour. The Swedish generals captured at Steinau were set free, among them Thurn whom Vienna regarded, rightly, as the leader of the Bohemian rebellion of 1618 and the most implacable enemy of the house of Habsburg. Wallenstein's reason, or pretext, for this show of clemency was the surrender of the Silesian fortresses in Swedish hands. At the same time Wallenstein challenged the powerful Spanish party. A Spanish army under the Duke of Feria had reached Tirol and was on its way against the Swedes under Horn who had occupied Swabia and Alsace and were besieging Constance and Breisach. Feria requested the help of a contingent of Wallenstein's army which was operating in Swabia under field-marshal Aldringen. Against Wallenstein's express order Aldringen joined Feria – an ominous sign of Wallenstein's declining authority. Feria and Aldringen relieved the besieged fortresses. This success, however, was annulled when a fortnight later (14 November) Bernard of Weimar forced the Bavarian garrison of Regensburg to capitulate after a brief siege. The imperial city joined the Heilbronn league and Bernard occupied Lower Bavaria as far as the Austrian frontier. The Emperor and Maximilian of Bavaria clamoured for Wallenstein's help. Wallenstein left Silesia in forced marches, reached Bernard's outposts in the Upper Palatinate – and returned to Bohemia where he made Pilsen his headquarters for the winter. Despite Ferdinand's urgent requests to move the billets into enemy territory, despite Maximilian's entreaties to liberate Bavaria, Wallenstein did not stir. Wallenstein's undisclosed motives may have been mixed: revenge for the humiliation he had suffered at Maximilian's hands in 1630, the desire to demonstrate his indispensability to Ferdinand, perhaps a genuine military need to rehabilitate his troops, and probably the wish to use the central position of Pilsen for continuing his devious negotiations with the Swedes, Saxons, French and Bernard. Whatever the true reasons for his inaction at this crucial moment, his fate was sealed.

On the one hand, Wallenstein at last decided openly to break with the Emperor, and to use his army, in conjunction with Saxony, Brandenburg, Sweden and France, to force peace upon Ferdinand. On the other hand, Ferdinand was now resolved to deprive Wallenstein of his command and to place the army under loyal generals.

On 11–13 January 1634 Wallenstein summoned his leading officers to Pilsen and made them swear unconditional allegiance to himself. Exaggerated reports of what was in itself a conspiracy, if not high treason, made Ferdinand take the final step. On 24 January he issued a secret decree which dismissed Wallenstein from the command, appointed Gallas as generalissimo and promised amnesty to the conspirators of Pilsen, Wallenstein and his two closest plotters excepted. Some of Wallenstein's generals had already been won over, among them Aldringen, Gallas and Piccolomini; even Seni, Wallenstein's trusted astrologer, was in Gallas's pay. An oral order given to the loyal generals on the same day instructed them to take the ringleaders prisoner 'if possible', or else 'to kill them as convicted criminals'.

Four weeks passed; both Wallenstein and the imperialist generals were hesitant and undecided. On 18 February the

Emperor issued an irrevocable 'patent of proscription' which was immediately publicized. Wallenstein's officers and troops deserted their general, almost without an exception. Wallenstein himself fled with some 1,500 men from Pilsen to the Bohemian frontier fortress of Eger and sent frantic appeals for help to Arnim and Bernard. Neither of them was eager to risk their troops or their reputation for an obviously lost cause. On 25 February 1634, Wallenstein's last four friends were assassinated during a banquet given in their honour by the treacherous commandant of Eger, the Scottish Lieutenant-Colonel John Gordon, in collusion with the Irish Colonel Walter Butler and the Scottish Major of Cavalry Walter Leslie. The actual murderers were Scottish, Irish, English and German officers and other ranks. One of these ruffians, the Irish Captain Walter Deveroux, broke into Wallenstein's bedroom and stabbed him to death.

The assassination was not only quite unnecessary but a serious mistake. A trial of Wallenstein and his fellow-conspirators would have revealed their secret dealings with the enemy, which often bordered on, and nearly always could be construed as, high treason. The 'military execution', as Butler and Leslie brazenly described the murder, supplied pamphleteers and journalists all over Europe with excellent propaganda material. The disregard of legal procedure was ascribed to the autocratic tendencies of the Emperor and the pernicious influence in German affairs of Spaniards and Jesuits. Father Joseph declared Oñate the main instigator, and Richelieu's newspapers blamed the Emperor for having removed by this '*acte sanglant*' the man who was about to give peace to Europe. Even at the court and in the army voices were raised in Wallenstein's defence, especially as the most diligent search failed to produce any conclusive proofs of the general's guilt, whereas the shameless greed with which Piccolomini, Gallas, Hatzfeld and their accomplices enriched themselves incensed many honest adherents of the imperial cause. In fact, out of the colossal confiscations of the rebel property, the imperial exchequer obtained least. The huge estates and immense funds were squandered among the generals and courtiers who had the ear of the weak and spendthrift Emperor. Down to 1918 a large part of the Austrian aristocracy lived on these rewards of their ancestors' loyalty to the house of Habsburg.

The imperial army was placed under the nominal command of the king of Hungary, Ferdinand III; the actual direction lay with the experienced South-Tirolese Gallas, now lord of the Wallenstein duchy of Friedland. The governor-designate of the Spanish Netherlands, the Cardinal-Infant Ferdinand, was on his way from Milan with a strong Spanish army. The two cousins and brothers-in-law outmanoeuvred Horn and Bernard, whose incompatibility anyway frustrated whole-hearted co-operation. The destruction of the Bavarian army at Landshut, where Aldringen was killed, was far outweighed by the loss of Regensburg and Donauwörth, which Ferdinand of Hungary recovered a few days later (July). The Swedes had been obliged to dispatch large forces against Poland after the Russian with-drawal from the war of Smolensk. The two Ferdinands therefore were vastly superior – about 35,000 against 20,000 men – when the armies met in the front of Nördlingen, the most formidable fortress-town in Swabia. In a fierce two-day battle (5–6 September 1634) the Swedes suffered a crushing defeat. Horn was taken prisoner, and the whole of South Germany was occupied by the victors. The Cardinal-Infant went on to Brussels where he shed his clerical garb and proved himself a competent military and civil administrator.

Bernard of Weimar escaped to Frankfurt with a handful of survivors from the disaster of Nördlingen. Here the military collapse was paralleled by the political break-up of the Heilbronn league. Even before the battle, Oxenstierna was faced by growing opposition to his leadership. Nearly all his allies in North Germany rallied to the peace proposals submitted by Saxony; these met most of the Emperor's demands and paid little regard to Swedish war-aims. When Oxenstierna disclosed the Swedish claims to Pomerania, Brandenburg went over to the Saxon party. The Heilbronn alliance was already in dissolution when the news of Nördlingen scattered the delegates. The Swedish pre-ponderance in Germany was finished. Its place was taken by France. Circumstances rather than inclination forced Richelieu and Feuquières to abandon their cautious manoeuvres behind the scenes and come into the open. On 28 April 1635, a fresh alliance between France and Sweden was concluded at Com-piègne, superseding the treaty of Bärwalde, and on 19 May France declared war on Spain.

With scant regard for Sweden and none for France, Saxony pursued the peace policy. The preliminary treaty of Pirna (24 November 1634) was still within the framework of the conditions on which Arnim and Wallenstein had agreed in 1633. The final peace of Prague (30 May 1635) revised them entirely in the Emperor's favour. The political clauses firmly established the Emperor's authority. All alliances between the Estates of the Empire were strictly forbidden. All armed forces were to be welded into an imperial army, paid by the Estates but administered by imperial commissaries; the Electors were to command their contingents as imperial generals. The reform of the imperial law courts and the aulic council was deferred to a future imperial diet; complaints about outlawry and confiscations were to be decided by the Emperor. No general amnesty was to be proclaimed; the Bohemian rebels were expressly excluded from any amnesty; the landgrave of Hesse–Cassel and the dukes of Weimar were promised forgiveness if they accepted the peace; otherwise the Emperor reserved to himself the right of granting or withholding clemency. The Palatinate was to remain in Maximilian's hands, Württemberg and Baden in imperial administration. Mecklenburg and Pomerania, in which the Emperor was not interested, were respectively to be restored to its dukes and promised to Brandenburg.

The edict of restitution was repealed, but only for forty years when the Emperor would regain his freedom of decision. During these forty years the Lutherans were allowed to retain the ecclesiastical lands which had been in their possession on 12 November 1627. The Calvinists were again excluded from these regulations. The 'ecclesiastical reservation' remained in force, the Protestant administrators of bishoprics remained debarred from the imperial diet. The archbishopric of Magdeburg was ceded for life to a younger son of John George of Saxony, the bishopric of Halberstadt was conferred on a younger son of the Emperor, that of Hildesheim on a Bavarian prince.

Neither the Emperor nor the Elector had consulted with a single prince, but the treaty was to have the force of a law passed by the imperial diet. The only oblique reference to Sweden was a passage which pledged all signatories to support the Emperor against any power that would oppose the peace. This was enough for Arnim to quit the Saxon service as he did not wish to fight against his erstwhile allies.

The peace of Prague was accepted by Bavaria, Saxony, Brandenburg, Mainz, Cologne, Trier (after Spanish soldiers had kidnapped the francophile archbishop), the landgrave of Hesse–

Darmstadt, the dukes of Mecklenburg and some imperial cities, including Lübeck, Frankfurt and Ulm. However, it failed to achieve a general pacification as its true intent only stiffened the determination of the anti-Habsburg powers, France, Sweden and the Netherlands.

## *The War of Smolensk*

Gustavus's and Richelieu's efforts to fight the Habsburg powers in central and western Europe were paralleled by their attempts to build up an alliance in eastern Europe, aimed chiefly against Poland and Austria. The French and Swedish envoys in Moscow came to an arrangement with the regent Philaret. Sweden and France also counted upon George Rákóczy (1631–48), Gabriel Bethlen's successor as prince of Transylvania; he was eager to resume Bethlen's policy in Hungary. In addition, it was hoped to obtain the co-operation of the Turkish Sultan, and to stir up the Tartars of the Crimea and the Cossacks of the Ukraine against their Polish overlords.

However, the scheme was too grandiose for speedy and concerted realization. The Sultan was involved in a long war with Persia (1630–38) and looked askance at the ambitious schemes of his Transylvanian vassal. The Tartars and Cossacks regarded the Russians rather than the Poles as their principal enemies; the Tartars actually turned their arms against Muscovy instead of Poland, and the Cossacks delayed their revolt until it was too late.

Only Russia acted. At first her contribution to the Swedish war effort was indirect. From 1628 to 1633 the Russian Government sold to Sweden large consignments of grain at an artificially low price. These shipments were resold by Sweden in the Amsterdam market at a considerable profit. It has been computed that each year the Russian exchequer received from the Swedes about 100,000 talers whereas the Swedes made about 400,000 talers from the resale. Military operations, however, started as late as the autumn of 1632 when the succession to the Polish throne of Wladislaw IV (1632–48), the erstwhile 'tsar' of Russia, gave added zest to Russian bellicosity – they hoped to recover the tracts east of the river Dniepr which Poland had wrenched from Muscovy during the 'time of troubles'. The Russians invaded Poland and laid siege to the town of Smolensk. Wrangel, the Swedish commander in Prussia, was ordered to advance in support of the

Russians. Gustavus himself may have planned, after having cleared Wallenstein out of Saxony, to march eastwards. The king's death, followed a year later (1 October 1633) by that of the Patriarch Philaret, removed the two principal architects of the Russo–Swedish alliance. Both Oxenstierna and Prince Tsher-kassky, who directed Russian policy after Philaret's death, had always been averse to it. Wladislaw's superior tactics and a dangerous rising of the peasants in central Russia forced the Russian government to break off the war. Swedish military assistance appeared too late on the Polish theatre of war; but their absence from Horn's army in south Germany was a fatal contribution to the disaster of Nördlingen. In June 1634 the tsar had to sign the peace of Polyanovka. Wladislaw formally renounced his claim to the Russian throne, but Poland kept Smolensk. A year later Sweden concluded the twenty-year truce of Stuhmsdorf with Poland. In return for the cession of Livonia, Sweden evacuated the Prussian ports. As in the west, so in the east, Sweden's position was showing ominous signs of overstrain.

### The Franco-Swedish Conflict with Austria-Spain

In 1635–36 Richelieu's diplomats were active all over Europe. An offensive and defensive alliance with the Netherlands (25 February) envisaged common action against the Spanish Nether-lands; the treaty of Compiègne (28 February) cemented the Swedish alliance; agreements with Savoy, Mantua and Parma (July) were designed to engage Spain and Austria in northern Italy; the mediation of the truce of Stuhmsdorf (12 September) separated Poland from the imperial cause. Finally, on 27 October, Bernard of Weimar and his army were enticed to enter the service of France.

These diplomatic successes and prospects were all the more vital for France as her military situation in 1635 and the first half of 1636 was precarious. The French declaration of war on Spain (19 May) was answered by a Spanish offensive: the archbishopric of Trier was overrun, Gallas invaded Lorraine and the Franche–Comté, and Piccolomini carried his arms almost to the gates of Paris (July 1636). Then, the tide began to turn. Bernard's operations between the French frontier and the Rhine were indecisive but prevented Gallas from intervening in north Germany. Here Banér and Torstenson had inflicted upon the

Saxon army a series of defeats (November–December 1635) which restored Swedish ascendancy. A year later, the two generals, ably assisted by the Scots, Alexander Leslie and James King, smashed at Wittstock in Brandenburg (4 October 1636) a combined imperialist and Saxon army under Count Hatzfeld. The whole of Pomerania, Brandenburg, Saxony and Thuringia were again in Swedish hands.

In 1637 the co-operation of the French and Dutch in the southern Netherlands began to bear fruit. The French started the conquest of the Artois, the Dutch took Breda and occupied a broad strip of the Spanish Netherlands from the Scheldt to the Meuse, later called the Generality Lands.

The only success the Spaniards achieved was the recovery of the Grisons. Here Rohan in 1635 defeated two Austrian and Spanish armies and reconquered the Valtellina. But Richelieu, curiously short-sighted, rejected Rohan's plea to place the Valtellina under Grisons jurisdiction. Unwilling to submit to French rule, Jenatsch entered into secret negotiations with the Spanish and Austrian governors of Milan and Innsbruck. In March 1637 a general rising took the French garrisons unprepared; they had to leave the Grisons. Blood-vengeance claimed Jenatsch as its victim: he was assassinated by the nephew of Pompejus Planta (24 January 1639). Agreements with Spain (1639) and Austria (1641) secured the nominal independence of the Grisons; but the vital passes came under Spanish control.

However, the secure passage across the Alps came too late to procure for the Spaniards the hoped-for military superiority in Germany and the Netherlands. Co-operation between Bernard and Banér, it is true, proved as difficult as that between Bernard and Horn had been. Gallas therefore ventured to neglect Bernard and undertook a raid against Banér who had to abandon some of the conquests made after Wittstock. But this departure of the imperialist forces gave Bernard the opportunity to prepare undisturbed his most brilliant campaign. In January 1638 he suddenly broke forth from his winter quarters near Basel, destroyed a joint imperialist-Bavarian army, capturing all the generals, and took the fortresses of Rheinfelden, Neuenburg, Freiburg and Breisach. The siege of Breisach lasted from June till December; several relieving forces were annihilated. The future marshal Turenne, leader of the French auxiliaries, here first showed his military genius. The occupation of the Breisgau

and Alsace effectively interrupted the Spanish highroad to the
Netherlands and gave Bernard his longed-for 'duchy of Alsace'.
But before he could reach agreement with Richelieu about the
final position of the duchy – whether as a French fief or as an
independent principality of the Empire – Bernard succumbed to
a bout of smallpox, not yet 35 years old (18 July 1639). His
victories gave France a firm foothold inside Germany. His
lieutenant-general, the Bernese patrician Hans Ludwig von
Erlach, sold Bernard's army with the towns and districts in its
possession to France.

The later career of Bernard showed that after the dissolution
of the Heilbronn alliance, any prospect of a purposeful direction
of the war in Germany had vanished. Oxenstierna lacked the
authority of Gustavus: the German princes refused to take orders
from a Swedish nobleman, and Swedish generals were not always
willing to obey one of their compeers. Even within the Swedish
government his position gradually weakened. The appointment
of his son Johan – an arrogant youth who showed no trace of his
father's genius – as a councillor of state aroused ill-feeling among
the aristocrats who did not belong to the Oxenstierna group.
When the chancellor's brother Gabriel died in the same year
(1640), the Oxenstiernas lost their majority in the council; and
when the diet declared Queen Christina of age on her eighteenth
birthday (1644), Oxenstierna's influence was further reduced.

Each of the Swedish generals therefore operated more or less
on his own responsibility, sometimes in conjunction, sometimes
almost in conflict with one another or the French or such German
princes as were still in arms. Their campaigns were largely dictated by the hope of financial gain and comfortable quarters;
Banér, like Bernard, seems to have aspired to a German principality but died in his 45th year (1641). Thereafter Torstenson
proved himself the greatest pupil of Gustavus. In a series of
lightning campaigns, undertaken regardless of season and
weather, he defeated one imperial army after another and carried
the war deep into the Habsburg crown lands of Bohemia, Silesia,
Moravia. His most spectacular victories were gained over the
most renowned imperial generals. Piccolomini was beaten in the
second battle of Breitenfeld (1642); Gallas failed to interrupt
Torstenson's Danish campaign (see below); Hatzfeld's army was
annihilated at Jankov in central Bohemia (1645). Exploiting this
triumph, Torstenson appeared before Krems, Vienna and Brno.

This campaign was concerted with Rákóczy, who in 1643 had been given the Sultan's permission to conclude an alliance with Sweden and France. Rákóczy overran Hungary as far as the river Waag, everywhere welcomed by the Protestant population. But the Sultan forbade further advances, and Rákóczy made his peace with the Emperor (August 1645). He retained most of his conquests and secured freedom of worship for the Protestants in the Habsburg portion of Hungary. Torstenson, for many years debilitated by arthritis, transferred the supreme command in Germany to Karl Gustaf Wrangel, who had taken a conspicuous part in the victory of Jankov.

The French generals, who took over Bernard's mercenaries and painfully built up a national French army, were under closer control. But they – and the Paris government – were chiefly interested in the war against Spain. The campaigns in Germany were of importance only so far as they assisted in interrupting the supply-line to the Spanish Netherlands. Only once marshal Guébriant advanced as far as Thuringia and once as far as Regensburg, both expeditions undertaken in conjunction with Banér and both without tangible results. In 1642 and 1643 Guébriant and Condé gained decisive victories over the Spaniards in the Netherlands. The destruction of the largest and last Spanish army in the battle of Rocroy (19 May 1643) marked the end of Spanish military greatness. Its immediate result was the overthrow of Olivárez and, with it, the termination of his aggressive policy. For in the same years the Dutch were also successfully invading the Spanish-Portuguese overseas possessions in Ceylon, the Gold Coast, northern Brazil, Malacca; and the last sizable Spanish armada, on its way to Antwerp, was destroyed in the English Channel (October 1639). Worst of all, two revolts in the Iberian peninsula shook the very foundations of Spanish power – with French help, first Catalonia, then Portugal rose in 1640. The Catalan rising was eventually suppressed, but Portugal regained her ancient independence. The first Braganza king at once concluded military and commercial treaties with France and Sweden.

In Germany, the position of the house of Habsburg took a similar turn for the worse. Brandenburg, under its new ruler Frederick William (1640–88), broke away from the Emperor and signed a truce with Sweden; Saxony followed suit shortly afterwards (1644–45). The landgravine Amalia, widow of William V of Hesse-Cassel, remained the most reliable and most efficient ally of Sweden. Maximilian of Bavaria was almost the only prince on whom the Emperor could rely. The combined imperialist and Bavarian troops were therefore the last line of defence. They inflicted a defeat on Turenne at Mergentheim in Franconia (May 1645) but three months later were decisively beaten by Turenne and Condé at Alerheim in Swabia. In the next year Turenne and Wrangel invaded Bavaria. The storming of Bregenz in Vorarlberg by Wrangel marked the southernmost point the Swedes ever reached. Maximilian concluded an armistice with France and Sweden; but, after the enemy had left Bavaria, imperialist troops forced Maximilian back to the Emperor's side. A fresh invasion by Turenne and Wrangel followed in the spring of 1648; the imperialist-Bavarian army was crushed at Zusmarshausen. Shortly afterwards the last troops the Emperor could afford to send to the aid of the Spaniards were wiped out by Condé at Lens in Artois. The last military exploit was the conquest of Hradčin castle and the surrounding district of Prague by a Swedish army under general Königsmark and the heir presumptive to the Swedish throne, the Count Palatine Charles Gustavus.

## *The Swedish–Danish War*

The numerous and expensive overseas commitments did not prevent the Swedish council of state from embarking on a fresh adventure, an attack upon Denmark. On the contrary, Sweden's increasing dependence upon France encouraged the council to look elsewhere for economic and territorial expansion. The oppressive duties which the Danish administration levied on the shipping passing through the Sound seriously impaired Swedish trade with the North Sea. They were equally obnoxious to the steadily growing Dutch and English trade with the Baltic countries.

Christian of Denmark's repeated attempts to subject the imperial city of Hamburg to Danish control added to the anxiety of Denmark's neighbours. For the neutrality of Hamburg was vital for the commercial relations with nominally hostile as well as supposedly friendly countries, which all belligerents maintained throughout the wars. Thus, for instance, the highly developed Dutch chemical industry (if this modern term may be used) was dependent on the import of alum, of which the mines of Tolfa in the papal states had the then world monopoly – since the 1570s, when direct traffic with the rebels against the Catholic Majesty would have been indiscreet, the papal administration shipped the alum to Lutheran Hamburg for re-export to Calvinist Amsterdam.

Christian's ruthless proceedings against Hamburg in May 1643 seem to have finally decided the Swedish council of state. Torstenson was ordered to break off his victorious campaign in Moravia and to turn against Denmark. Within a few weeks his troops covered about 500 miles, overran Schleswig-Holstein and marched into Jutland. At the same time Horn, who had been released from captivity in 1642, invaded the Danish provinces in southern and western Sweden. A fleet was chartered in Holland, which cleared the Baltic and facilitated the capture of the isolated Danish islands of Gotland and Oesel. An imperialist army under Gallas was ordered to relieve the Danes. Torstenson turned about, destroyed Gallas's troops in two battles at Jüterbog and Magdeburg and resumed his warfare in Bohemia.

The peace of Brömsebro (25 August 1645) obliged Denmark to cede to Sweden the islands of Oesel and Gotland and the districts of Jämtland, Härjedalen and Halland. The possession of Halland safeguarded the hitherto isolated port of Göteborg: Sweden's access to Western Europe was secure.

Hamburg, which had paid considerable subsidies into the Swedish war-chest, was admitted to the benefits which Sweden and the Netherlands obtained in the commercial sphere. It is significant that the post of Spanish resident which Gabriel de Roy had filled from 1630 was now moved from Glückstadt to Hamburg. The Sound duties were lowered to the modest level of 1603; the signatories were exempted from the Glückstadt duties. The Netherlands, Hamburg and Bremen moreover concluded a treaty for the protection of shipping on the rivers Elbe, Weser and in the North Sea. Denmark was reduced to a second-rate power in both northern waters.

## The Peace of Westphalia

All the major and minor wars that since 1609 had flared up in one part or another of central and eastern Europe were terminated by treaties of truce or peace. To call to mind this series, from the Spanish-Dutch truce of 1609 to the Swedish-Danish peace of 1645 is in itself sufficient to discredit the lingering con-concept of a single 'Thirty Years War'.

However, these earlier peace treaties were essentially *ad hoc* arrangements. They largely ignored the European character of all these conflicts and therefore left unsolved almost as many problems as they tried to settle. Consequently the peace of West-phalia, which ended the war between the French-Swedish-Dutch alliance and the Spanish-Austrian bloc, aimed at a compre-hensive composition of all outstanding points at issue. Hence the long duration of the peace congress and the slow and tortuous progress of its deliberations, caused by the intertwining and over-lapping problems on its agenda.

Several changes among the leading personalities in the years around 1640 either speeded or retarded the peace negotiations. In 1637 the Emperor Ferdinand II died. His eldest son, Ferdinand III, had in the previous year at last been elected king of the Romans (though still against the opposition of Bavaria and the Curia) and now succeeded him, with none of the Electors dis-senting. Unlike his father, the new Emperor was always prepared to abandon positions which his realistic mind recognized as untenable. In order to maintain and strengthen his absolute power in the hereditary crown lands of the house of Austria, he felt few if any qualms in bartering away what had been dearest to his father's heart: the unity of the church, the integrity of the Empire and the interests of the Spanish Habsburgs.

The accession to power of Cardinal Mazarin on the death of Richelieu (1642) gave a new turn, or at least a different em-phasis, to French policy. During the minority of the new king, Louis XIV, Mazarin was the sole director of French affairs until his death (1661). Contrary to Richelieu's far-sighted concepts of the concert of Europe, the Italian-born Mazarin took a narrowly French view of European problems. This attitude soon roused the suspicion of the Dutch statesmen who began to see the greater danger in an aggressive France rather than a decaying Spain. The overthrow of Olivárez opened the door to an honourable conclusion of the Eighty Years War.

The coming of age of Gustavus Adolphus's daughter, Christina, in 1644 shook the exclusive rule of the high aristocracy in Sweden. The young queen took an active part in the deliberations of the council of state. In opposition to the civilian and military noblemen who regarded the war as a profitable business to fill their own pockets, Christina worked for peace – at almost any price. The sacrifices in blood and money which the mass of the population had to bear made her attitude very popular. In Adler Salvius, a man of low birth, Christina found a skilful and determined advocate of her policy, capable of holding his own against the bellicose and selfish nobility.

Among the German princes, the assumption of the regency in Hesse-Cassel by the landgravine Amalia (1637) and the accession of Frederick William in Brandenburg (1640) brought to the fore two energetic Calvinist princes who completely overshadowed John George of Saxony, who still pursued his equivocal policy of appeasement. In the Catholic camp, the vacillations of Maximilian of Bavaria during the years 1646–48 showed that the ageing Elector was losing his firm grasp, although in the end he returned to the French allegiance.

On the other hand, France lost a valuable ally when Pope Urban VIII died in 1644. He had been an unswerving opponent of the Habsburgs, but the growing preponderance of France in the affairs of Italy made a determined minority of the cardinals anxious to restore the equilibrium. They defeated the pro-French majority in a long-drawn ballot and their victorious candidate Innocent X (1644–55) reversed his predecessor's policy in favour of Spain.

The first steps towards the peace which was eventually concluded in 1648 were taken in 1638. The Hamburg treaty, signed on 6 March by the Count d'Avaux for France and by Adler Salvius for Sweden, bound the signatories to make peace only in common. The congress was to meet in two places, France and Sweden respectively presiding; the originally proposed cities of Cologne and Hamburg were later, in 1641, replaced by Catholic Münster and Protestant Osnabrück which recommended themselves because of their proximity. The aims were the restitution of the political, constitutional and religious status of 1618, a general amnesty, and the 'satisfaction' of the 'two crowns' of France and Sweden. At the same time Ferdinand III sounded the possibility of a separate peace with Sweden. But the Swedish council of state flatly rejected the Emperor's proposals and indeed any separate negotiations with him.

At a meeting of the Emperor with the Electors in Nürnberg (1640), Ferdinand realized that the Electors were willing to fall in with the basic demands of France and Sweden. As a counter-stroke he summoned the imperial diet which had not met for nearly thirty years. Ferdinand hoped to mobilize the lesser princes against the Electors, but the diet expressed its longing for peace in declarations which corresponded completely with the wishes of the two crowns.

After three more years of half-hearted and inconclusive discussions and correspondence between all parties, the tireless exertions of the landgravine Amalia played a decisive part in overcoming the hesitancy of some, the obstinacy of others, and the backstairs intrigues of all. The final invitations, issued by France and Sweden to all Estates of the Empire in September–October 1644, were accepted, last of all by the Emperor. While the ambassadors of the Estates were gradually assembling in Münster and Osnabrück, the Emperor conceded that a general amnesty was to be promulgated, and all Estates should be admitted as fully qualified representatives of the Empire and as independent members of the society of European states.

The congress as a whole and its two sections at Münster and Osnabrück were never formally opened or constituted, but from the middle of 1645 the negotiations were in full swing. In December 1645 the Swedes and French for the first time made known their demands which were to underpin the 'restitution of the German liberty' as they continued to describe their war-aim. Some of their demands were clearly meant only to be used for bargaining purposes. The Swedes demanded the whole of Pomerania (whose last duke had died in 1637) and Silesia, the bishoprics of Bremen, Verden, Magdeburg, Halberstadt, Kammin, Minden and Osnabrück, the port of Wismar, and a 'satisfaction' for their army; this was to consist of 9 to 12 million talers or even 20 million, if Silesia and some of the bishoprics were unobtainable. The Swedes could not have asked for more, the imperial ambassador exclaimed, if the Emperor were a prisoner in Stockholm.

The French territorial demands looked modest by comparison. They comprised the bishoprics of Metz, Toul and Verdun, which had been French protectorates since 1552; the districts on both sides of the upper Rhine which Bernard of Weimar had conquered in Richelieu's pay; and the fortress of Philippsburg in the bishopric of Speier. In reality, however, the French proposals were kept studiously vague and thus paved the way for the extravagant interpretation later put upon them by Louis XIV's 'chambers of reunion'. Thus the three Lorraine 'episco-patus' could be understood as meaning either the temporal possessions of the bishops, or the whole dioceses in their spiritual charge; and the latter might be taken to include even the secular fiefs, such as the large Protestant counties of Saarbrücken and Zweibrücken. Similarly, the term Upper and Lower Alsace comprised a medley of secular and ecclesiastical imperial fiefs, imperial cities and imperial villages and perhaps the bishopric of Strasbourg; the feudal nexus of all these petty sovereignties was ill-defined and virtually indefinable.

It was taken for granted by every participant of the congress that the German Empire was to square the reckoning in full. Two territories which were still nominally member states of the Empire, the Netherlands and Switzerland, therefore made haste to dissociate themselves formally from the Empire. The recog-nition in international law of Dutch independence was at once admitted by the Spaniards, as soon as the representatives of the United Provinces declared their willingness to abandon the French alliance and to conclude a separate peace with Spain. The inevitable consent of the Emperor and Empire was cloaked in the meaningless proviso that the ultimate fate of the 'Burgundian circle' should be left in suspense until a Spanish-French peace be signed. In fact, the conclusion of the Dutch-Spanish peace on 30 January 1648 ended the Eighty Years War and separated the Netherlands for good from the German Empire.

The Swiss Confederation had come through the wars of the past forty years without being involved in any of them. The Grisons, it must be remembered, repeatedly the theatre of war, was a loose ally but not a member of the League. Swiss neutrality was as much the result of prudent statesmanship as of the impossibility of devising a consistent policy out of the discordant political, religious and economic interests of the thirteen cantons. The Confederation was therefore not invited to the peace congress, and its exclusion was accepted almost gratefully by the Roman Catholic cantons which were unwilling to side with or against Austria, Spain or France. However, when the annexionist plans of France became known, the city of Basel took alarm; for it would have been almost encircled by a series of French fort-resses. The Roman Catholic cantons still objected to attending the peace congress, but the Protestant cantons sent the Basel burgomaster Johann Rudolf Wettstein as their plenipotentiary to Münster. Wettstein achieved his aim. A clause in the peace treaty formally 'exempted' 'the city of Basel and the other Swiss cantons' from their obligations towards the Empire.

The aversion to becoming implicated in the dismemberment of the Empire was also uppermost in the thoughts of the Emperor, who ought to have acted as the principal spokesman of its interest. Ferdinand III and his advisers were determined that whoever was to lose territory, to abandon principles, to pay indemnities, it should not be the house of Austria. In order to prevent the Electors and the other Estates from signing the peace without the Emperor, Ferdinand abandoned the Spanish alliance and accepted the religious compromises on which the Protestant and Catholic Estates had agreed. In order to keep Silesia and to exclude the Protestants of the Austrian crownlands from the religious toleration accorded to their coreligionists in the Empire, Ferdinand sacrificed Pomerania and the north German bishoprics to the Swedes and their German partisans. In order to keep the Breisgau and the upper Rhenish fortresses of Laufenburg and Rheinfelden, he offered France Upper and Lower Alsace and the imperial cities and bishoprics of Metz, Toul and Verdun. The fortress of Breisach was the only direct loss Austria suffered, for the Emperor's feudal rights in Alsace and Lorraine were so nugatory that Ferdinand gave up little. From the French point of view, two main advantages resulted from these acquisitions: Alsace and Lorraine were sure to fall sooner or later under French dominion; and the garrisoning of Breisach and Philippsburg laid south Germany open to French invasion. France owed its success not least to the pressure which Maximilian of Bavaria exerted upon the Emperor on behalf of his French allies. He therefore benefited to the extent that he was confirmed in his electoral dignity and allowed to keep the Upper Palatinate. Moreover he saved Paderborn for his brother Ferdinand and Osnabrück for Ferdinand's bastard Wartenberg: Hesse-Cassel had wanted to annex the one bishopric, the Guelphs the other.

The Swedes had to abandon some of the extreme demands of the war party. Above all, the acquisition of the whole of Pomerania proved impossible in the face of the determined opposition of Frederick William of Brandenburg. His hereditary rights to the duchy would have availed him nothing; but Denmark, Poland and the Netherlands did not wish to see the entire Baltic coast in Swedish hands and therefore supported Brandenburg. In the end, Pomerania was divided: Sweden obtained the more valuable Western Pomerania with Stralsund, Greifswald, Stettin, the islands of Rügen, Usedom and Wollin, and a tract on the right bank of the river Oder; whereas Brandenburg received Eastern Pomerania with the bishopric of Kammin, which included Kolberg as the only port of any significance. This compromise was offset by the gains of both elsewhere: Sweden acquired the Mecklenburg port of Wismar and the bishoprics of Bremen and Verden, comprising the whole country between the lower Elbe and lower Weser; the mouths of the rivers Oder, Elbe and Weser, controlling the German commerce towards the Baltic and North Seas, were firmly in Swedish hands. Brandenburg received large compensations: the archbishopric of Magdeburg was to go to Brandenburg after the death of the present administrator, a Saxon prince; the bishoprics of Halberstadt and Minden and two Hartz counties nearly filled the gap between the Electorate and its Rhenish-Westphalian territories acquired from the Jülich inheritance. Brandenburg was definitely outstripping Saxony which only kept Lusatia (ceded by the peace of Prague) but obtained nothing further.

Two other adherents of Sweden, Brunswick-Lüneburg and Hesse-Cassel, were put off with minor gains that fell short of their expectations. Their disappointment was due mainly to the opposition of France and Bavaria, which did not wish to see powerful Protestant countries straddling north-west and west-central Germany.

All these gains and losses – including numerous minor adjustments – were determined entirely by the interests of the principal powers, France and Sweden. The genuine desire for peace, as well as the selfish ambitions of their respective partisans, gave the two crowns ample scope to harmonize their own, often seemingly insoluble differences at somebody else's expense, to reward the obedient or potentially useful, and to make the recalcitrant or negligible bear the cost of the final settlement.

However, the territorial acquisitions and cessions were not the only concern of the peace congress, or even the sole preoccupation of the two crowns and the Emperor. The peace of Westphalia finally settled the constitutional and religious problems which had for centuries beset the German Empire; and it settled them within a European framework.

The struggle between the monarchical and centralistic aspirations of the Emperor and the oligarchic and federalistic tendencies of the Estates was decided in favour of the latter. The edict of restitution and the peace of Prague – the highwater marks of imperial ascendancy – were repealed. The Estates were granted full sovereignty, including the right to conclude alliances among themselves and with foreign powers, limited only by the futile clause that such alliances must not be directed against the Emperor and Empire. The 'electoral pre-eminence' was eliminated; all Estates were regarded as equal – but France and Sweden saw to it that their supporters were more equal than the rest. The Emperor had to cede to the imperial diet the *jus pacis et belli*, i.e. the declaration of war, conclusion of peace, levying and quartering of troops, building and garrisoning of fortresses. The chief imperial institutions were henceforth to be composed on a footing of religious equality – the supreme court, for instance, was to consist of two Protestant and two Catholic presidents and 26 Catholic and 24 Protestant judges. Religious disputes brought before the imperial diet were no longer to be decided by majority vote, but by amicable settlement between the Corpus Catholicorum and the Corpus Evangelicorum, each formed *ad hoc* by the respective Estates whenever religious issues came under consideration.

This regulation was the cornerstone of the religious settlement. Credit for achieving compromises, which eventually proved more or less satisfactory to the great majority of all parties, is mainly due to the representatives of the Catholic bishops of Würzburg and Bamberg and of the Lutheran dukes of Brunswick and Weimar. The envoys of Brandenburg and Hesse-Cassel, supported by the Emperor's ambassador, achieved the admission of the Calvinists to the religious peace of Augsburg. A long quarrel developed over the question of the 'standard year', i.e. the date which should determine the position of the bishoprics, abbeys and secular countries which had adopted the reformed religion or been recatholicized. The Protestants wished to restore the conditions prevailing in 1618. The radical Catholics demanded the status of 1630. In the end the first of January 1624 was accepted. Some exceptions were made in favour of the Catholics in Austria, Bavaria and several imperial cities, above all Aachen. More important in the long run was the virtual abandonment by both parties of the maxim *Cujus regio ejus religio*. Henceforth the conversion of the ruler did not automatically oblige his subjects to accept his new creed; and dissident subjects were allowed private worship and the right to emigrate, again with the exception of the Habsburg dominions. The Protestant administrators of the reformed north-German bishoprics were at last admitted to the imperial diet with full voting rights.

Although all the religious clauses were hedged in on every side by conditions, reservations and exceptions, they marked a definite step towards the separation of politics and religion. Politics became secularized, religion was to be left to the conscience of the individual. That the negotiators of the peace of Westphalia were conscious of this trend – moreover, positively approved it – is clearly shown by their attitude towards the papacy. As at former international congresses, the Holy See was represented by two 'mediators', one of them the nuncio Chigi, later Pope Alexander VII, the other an experienced Venetian diplomatist. Their good intentions and zealous efforts, however, were frustrated from the beginning, because they were not permitted to have any direct dealings with the heretical envoys. Moreover, Chigi was the uneasy guardian of a secret papal breve, dated October 1644, which roundly condemned the toleration of any form of non-Roman Christianity and the cession of any church property to heretical rulers. In vain Chigi hoped that the papal protest would make the Catholic princes recoil from the implied threat of eternal damnation. Chigi's first intimation, in November 1647, was met with embarrassed, evasive and apologetic answers. His formal proclamation of the breve, on Christmas Eve, received the most mortifying rebuff, as none of the Catholic princes even deigned to acknowledge it. On the contrary, both the Catholic and Protestant envoys inserted in the peace a special 'anti-protest clause'; it bluntly stated that the papal condemnation of the peace was invalid and ineffectual. The official publication of the bull *Zelo Domus Dei*, dated 20 November 1648 but promulgated only on 3 January 1651, made no difference to the fact that the voice of the Supreme Pontiff counted for nothing in the chancelleries of Europe.

Chigi was equally unsuccessful with the similar papal protest against the Spanish-Dutch peace of 30 January. In order to spare the susceptibilities of the faithful court of Madrid, he entered the protest in form of a deposition before a notary and seven witnesses, all of whom were sworn to strictest secrecy (18 May 1648).

One of the most difficult questions to be settled was the financial 'satisfaction' of the Swedish army. In this respect Oxenstierna was not a free agent, as the generals put forth their and the soldiers' claim regardless of political considerations. The Estates of the Empire originally offered 1,600,000 talers against the Swedish demand for 20 million. Salvius (and Queen Christina) eventually lowered this sum to 5 million. This figure was accepted by the Estates; the Emperor's consent was bought by Swedish abandonment of the Austrian and Bohemian Protestants. Their confiscated estates were not returned to them and the denial of religious toleration in their home lands made them perpetual exiles – but they were now assured at least of a financial compensation as most of them were serving in the armies of the Swedes and their allies.

The signing of the peace treaty took place on 24 October 1648 in the lodgings of the imperial ambassador in Münster. It was ratified on 8 February 1649, when the peace was solemnly placed under the common guarantee of Sweden and France. Details of its execution were settled at a congress which sat in Nürnberg from April 1649 to June 1651. Here Piccolomini, representing the Emperor, showed himself a skilful diplomatist; he carried a number of interpretative amendments favourable to the house of Austria, for which Ferdinand raised him to the dignity of a prince of the Empire.

The peace of Westphalia remained in force until the end of the Holy Roman Empire in 1806. In its German as well as European aspects, it marked the end of the middle ages and heralded the era of the secular concert of Europe.

The growth of French influence upon the affairs of Europe manifested itself in the question of the languages used in the negotiations and the treaties. For a thousand years Latin had been the accepted language of international diplomacy. In Münster, the French delegation, from the beginning, employed only French in their written and oral communications. The Germans and the Swedes protested and demanded the use of Latin in writing and of Latin or German in discussions. In fact, the negotiations in Osnabrück were conducted in German whereas Latin, French and Italian were spoken in Münster. The Spaniards and Dutch agreed on French and Dutch as of equal right, with Latin as a subsidiary. Consequently, the treaties concluded with the emperor and empire were couched in Latin but all the others in French. French was to become increasingly the exclusive language of diplomacy until the peace of Versailles in 1919 when, for the first time, English obtained parity with, and subsequently predominance over French.

### The Franco-Spanish War

The comparatively speedy conclusion of the Dutch-Spanish peace of Münster (30 January 1648) was due to the willingness of both parties to reach a settlement upon the basis of compromise. The United Provinces realized that their independence was no longer threatened by the declining Spanish monarchy, but that they had now to guard against the expansive tendencies of France. The Spanish government, on its part, wished to turn the whole might of Spain against France. For the internal conditions of France gave Madrid some reasonable hope of restoring Spanish influence in Paris with the active assistance of at least a powerful section of Frenchmen themselves, as had happened in the second half of the sixteenth century before the accession of Henry IV.

From about 1645 the exactions of Mazarin's tax-officers were causing widespread unrest of which the cardinal and the queen-mother became the chief objects. The Parlements of Paris and Bordeaux made themselves the mouthpieces of popular dissatisfaction, adding constitutional demands to economic complaints. The anti-monarchical language used by the Parlements in 1646–48 was such as might be heard at Westminster; and the arrest of two members of the Paris Parlement by Queen Anne in August 1648 repeated Charles I's folly. However, Anne, warned by the sequel of Strafford's fate, refused to sacrifice Mazarin to the wrath of the Parlement. The opposition of the Parlement gained momentum when it was joined by the populace of Paris as well as by the high aristocracy. The leaders of the Fronde were princes of the blood royal: Prince Louis II de Condé, the most brilliant general of the French army, his brother Prince Armand de Conti and his brother-in-law Henry Duke of Longueville (who had been the principal French ambassador at the peace congress of Münster) – Mazarin compared them with Cromwell and Fairfax. After Condé, Conti and Longueville had been arrested, the Duchess of Longueville and Marshal Turenne, who had joined the Fronde, concluded a treaty with the king of

Spain, which postulated the liberation of the princes and the conclusion of a Franco-Spanish peace treaty (20 April 1650). When the heir presumptive, Duke Gaston of Orleans, joined the Fronde, Mazarin had to yield. The three princes were released and the Cardinal fled to Cologne (February 1651). But he continued to advise the queen-mother. The young king, Louis XIV, was declared of age on 5 September 1651 – a seeming formality, which however released Queen Anne from having to consult the princes of the blood royal.

In 1652 matters came to a head. Condé raised the standard of rebellion and entered into an open alliance with the Spaniards and Dutch. Spanish subsidies placed a Dutch army under his command; in return Condé promised to work for a 'good, just and secure' peace. On the royalist side Mazarin was recalled from his exile, bringing with him two valuable converts to the king's cause, Turenne and his brother, the duke of Bouillon. He soon succeeded in further disrupting the leadership of the Fronde by marrying his niece to Prince Conti and by reconciling the feckless Duke of Orleans. The war turned into a duel between Condé and Turenne. For a few months in the summer of 1652 Condé seemed to be supreme. He entered Paris and invited the Spaniards to join him there. The Spaniards occupied Gravelines and Dunkirk in Flanders, Noyon in Picardy and Casale in Piedmont, but failed to reach Paris.

Victory, however, rested with Mazarin and the king. The ultimate aims of the ambitious princes and the privileged bourgeoisie were irreconcilable; the latter objected especially to the appeasement of Spain. Paris, in October 1652, and Bordeaux, in August 1653, returned to the royal obedience. Moreover, the great majority of the army refused to join the rebel Condé, just as twenty years earlier the imperial army had refused to follow Wallenstein. The pull of legitimacy and the sanctity of the military oath also prevailed when in 1654 the governor of Alsace, the Lorraine Count Harcourt, turned against Mazarin, gained control of the fortresses of Philippsburg and Breisach, and opened negotiations with the Emperor and Spain. A latter-day Bernard of Weimar, Harcourt wanted to possess himself of an independent duchy, but his troops forsook him, and he had to submit to Mazarin.

Despite some reverses Turenne gradually expelled the Spaniards from northern France and advanced into the Spanish

Netherlands; the Catalan rebels and the Portuguese were sustained by French support; the French fleet inflicted a defeat on the Spaniards off Barcelona; Roussillon was occupied. From 1655 French superiority was assured. The final military decision, however, was brought about by England. The Spaniards were the first to solicit Cromwell's help for a concerted attack on France; Bordeaux was to be the English prize. But they declined Cromwell's two main demands: freedom of trade with the American colonies and freedom of worship for the English traders sojourning in Spanish territory. Cromwell therefore reverted to the Elizabethan anti-Spanish policy. Robert Blake's exploits in the Mediterranean and Caribbean seas, and the capture of Jamaica made Spain declare war on England (February 1656). Thereupon Cromwell concluded treaties of friendship and alliance with France. In the course of 1657–58 the English co-operated with the French under Turenne in conquering Mardyk, Dunkirk, Gravelines, Oudenaarde and Ypres. Dunkirk was at once handed over to England.

At the same time Mazarin strengthened his ties with the anti-Habsburg opposition of the German princes. He failed, it is true, to make Ferdinand Maria of Bavaria, Maximilian's weak successor, accept the offer of the imperial crown which France, Sweden and Brandenburg wanted to secure for him, first after the untimely death of the king of the Romans, Ferdinand IV (1654) and then on the demise of the Emperor Ferdinand III (1657). But the Electors, counselled by Mazarin, forced upon the new Emperor, Leopold 1, a 'capitulation' which obliged him to refrain from giving assistance to Spain – the traditional co-ordination of the policies of the two Habsburg branches was effectively broken. Four weeks after Leopold's election, the archbishops of Mainz, Cologne and Trier, the bishop of Münster, the count palatine of Neuburg, the duke of Brunswick-Lüneburg, the landgrave of Hesse-Cassel and the two crowns of France and Sweden concluded the 'Rhenish alliance' (14 August 1658). It was directed implicitly against the Emperor and Spain whom the German princes still considered their most formidable antagonists.

Once again, as with Gustavus Adolphus and Bernard of Weimar, the demise of an inconvenient ally benefited France. Oliver Cromwell's death (3 September 1658) freed Mazarin from the need of having to consider England in his dealings with Spain.

A few weeks later peace negotiations began in Lyon; they were eventually conducted by Mazarin and the Spanish minister Luis de Haro, who met from 13 August to 7 November 1659 on an islet in the Bidassoa river, a tiny plot of no-man's-land in the western Pyrenees. Spain's chief concession was a marriage contract between Louis XIV and Philip IV's daughter; the Spaniards had opposed it because they were afraid it might eventually lead to the Spanish crown devolving upon a Bourbon (as in fact it did in 1700); for the same reason the French insisted upon it. France abandoned the Catalan rebels and her alliance with Portugal, returned Franche-Comté and reinstated Condé in all his former dignities and possessions. Spain ceded Roussillon (thus making the ridge of the Pyrenees the permanent Franco–Spanish frontier), Artois (with its capital Arras), Gravelines, Montmédy, Thionville and other places in the Spanish Netherlands; it formally renounced its claim to Alsace and withdrew the Spanish garrison from Jülich. Both France and Spain were amenable to making the duke of Lorraine, Spain's unwavering ally, suffer the greatest losses: he had to surrender to France the fortresses of Stenay, Montmédy and Clermont and the Barrois, which bridged the gap between France and the three towns of Metz, Verdun and Toul; and to raze the fortifications of his capital, Nancy, making Lorraine completely defenceless.

The peace of the Pyrenees fulfilled the highest hopes Henry IV had entertained half a century earlier. Spain was reduced to a second-class power, soon to become the pawn in the game of European politics which she had dominated for a century and a half. Cromwell and the German princes, less far-sighted than the United Provinces, had misread the signs of the time, and helped to make France the undisputed master of Europe.

## The Nordic War

The decline of Spain was paralleled by the collapse of Poland. The reign of King John II Casimir (1648–68) began with a revolt of the Ukrainian Cossacks who allied themselves with the tsar of Muscovy. By 1654 the Russians had advanced all along their western frontier, taking Smolensk, Chernigov and Kiev. John Casimir chose this moment to renew the claims of the Polish Vasas to the Swedish throne. The extravagance of Queen Christina had depleted the royal treasury; tens of thousands of returned officers and soldiers were not yet re-integrated into the economic life of the country; the lavish grants to the generals and other noblemen had alienated over two-thirds of the productive land. The Polish provocation gave Charles X Gustavus (1654–60) an opportune pretext to extricate himself from these difficulties by a military diversion. Trained in Torstenson's school, he showed his military competence in a series of lightning campaigns which filled his short reign.

The simultaneous invasion of Poland by the Swedes, Russians and Cossacks all but brought about the dissolution of the state in 1654. But the very extent of the Swedish successes caused a reversal. The Russians were the first to turn their arms against their late allies; they were soon joined by the Austrians. Charles found an unexpected ally in Frederick William of Brandenburg. The Elector had been the first to try to upset the peace of Westphalia: in 1651 he suddenly attacked Jülich in an attempt to make himself master of Jülich-Berg. But the Estates of the duchy together with those of Cleves-Mark opposed him, and the Emperor, Spain and Poland forced him to retreat ignominiously. Now, in 1656, Frederick William concluded alliances with Sweden and France and in a three-day battle at Warsaw the Swedes and Brandenburgers defeated the Polish army. Under Austrian mediation Frederick William then changed sides, for which Poland rewarded him by resigning its feudal overlordship over Prussia (September 1657).

Incited by the Emperor, Spain and the United Provinces, Frederick III of Denmark (1648–70) thought the moment opportune to reverse the peace of Brömsebro. He attacked Sweden in May 1657, but Charles X defeated the Danes, and, in the peace of Roskilde (27 February 1658), forced them to cede all remaining Danish possessions in southern Sweden as well as the island of Bornholm and the district of Trondheim in central Norway; in addition, Sweden was freed from the payment of the Sound dues.

This brought about an anti-Swedish alliance of Austria, Poland, Brandenburg and the Netherlands. Charles again conquered the greater part of Denmark, but the allied land forces under the command of Frederick William expelled the Swedes from Jutland and Pomerania, a Dutch fleet forced Charles to raise the siege of Copenhagen, and the population of Bornholm and Trondheim rose against the Swedes. When a Dutch fleet transported the allied troops to the island of Fynen where they annihilated Charles's best army (November 1659), France intervened on behalf of her old ally. The invasion of Pomerania was declared a violation of the peace of Westphalia, which France as one of its guarantors was bound to uphold. Under French mediation the peace of Copenhagen was concluded between Sweden and Denmark, that of Oliva between Sweden and Poland (1660). Denmark recovered Bornholm and Trondheim but lost southern Sweden for good. Poland formally ceded Livonia, Estonia and Oesel, and John Casimir renounced all claims to the Swedish throne. Frederick William's sovereignty in Prussia was internationally recognized, but he had to abandon his chief war-aim, Swedish Pomerania.

The peace between Russia and Poland was signed much later (1667); it left unchanged the position Russia had acquired in 1654.

The Nordic War had momentous long-term results. France replaced the Netherlands in Sweden and Austria in Poland as the controlling foreign influence; and there had appeared on the political scene two newcomers, one of whom, Brandenburg-Prussia, was increasingly to determine the fate of Germany and Europe, and the other, Russia, that of Europe and the world.

# CHAPTER THREE

# *The Thirty Years War: Myth and Reality*

THE rejection of the traditional picture of the Thirty Years War as an unmitigated disaster is not based on the discovery of fresh sources, but largely on the experience of two world wars. This has supplied the historian of the mid-twentieth century with a new perspective and a deeper understanding than his pre-decessors could derive from a century of liberal, progressive ideology.

The propaganda by word of mouth and through the printing press as perfected during the Second World War has taught us how credulous even an educated and critical audience can become. The atrocity propaganda of the chopped-off hands of Belgian children in 1914 has given us a yardstick by which to measure the stories of cannibalism in the seventeenth century. The German inflation of 1919–23 has clarified the significance of the German inflation of 1619–22. The obliteration of Coventry, Hamburg and Dresden has shown us the real meaning of the word destruction – as well as the miraculous power of recovery and reconstruction. We now know something of the difficulties inherent in the transition from war to peace – and how convenient it is to shift the blame for the hardships of reconstruction from the incompetence of post-war politicians to the allegedly lasting effects of the war.

It is in the light of these experiences of our own time that the picture of the Thirty Years War must be recast.

It is not the purpose of the present chapter to glorify the Thirty Years War; and much misery, brutality, cruelty and suffering no doubt added to the terror and slaughter of purely military actions. But nothing is gained by putting the Thirty Years War in a class by itself. Its destructive aspects are common to every war – and were in any case smaller than those of 'total war' in the twentieth century – and some of the features commonly attributed to it are unconnected with the war itself, while others have been generalized and exaggerated. The generalization of isolated events, the exaggeration of facts and figures, the special pleading for a particular cause lay the contemporary chroniclers and diarists less open to criticism than those modern historians who have failed to recognize the distorted perspective from which these accounts were written.

## The Traditional Picture

The genealogy of the traditional picture of the 'Thirty Years War' as accepted uncritically for nearly three centuries, can be traced largely to the war- and post-war propaganda undertaken at the behest of the Swedish and Brandenburg governments. Already during the war Oxenstierna secured the services of the Pomeranian lawyer and historian Bogislav Philipp Chemnitz (1605–78). Appointed Swedish state historiographer in 1644, he wrote, under the pseudonym of Hippolithus a Lapide, an effective polemic against the centralizing tendencies of the house of Habsburg (*Dissertatio de ratione status in imperio nostro Romano-Germanico*, published in 1643 or 1646 but backdated 1640). Numerous Dutch reprints (all misdated 1641) spread Chemnitz's – or rather Oxenstierna's – ideas all over Europe and influenced the deliberation in Osnabrück. This pamphlet was followed by two volumes on 'the royal Swedish war in Germany' (1648 and 1653). Of far greater importance, however, were the writings of one of the most brilliant academic publicists of the age, the jurist and historian Samuel Pufendorf (1632–94). A native of Saxony, he was successively professor of international law at the universities of Heidelberg in the Palatinate and Lund in Sweden, and historiographer royal and privy counsellor to Charles XI of Sweden and Frederick William I of Brandenburg.

In the rather transparent guise of an Italian nobleman, Severinus de Monzambano, Pufendorf wrote a pamphlet *De statu imperii Germanici* (1667); it was immediately reprinted and, within two years, translated into German, French, English and Dutch and soon became the acknowledged textbook in Swedish and German universities. Here we find some of the main arguments of later writers: the Bohemian rebellion as the 'brand which set ablaze the whole of Germany'; the peace of Westphalia as the end of 'this war'; the religious differences as the main cause of the political dissensions, and the classification of Austria as one of the three 'foreign powers' which, like Turkey and France, might head an 'alliance against Germany'. These points thrown out as incidental glosses in this legal rather than historical pamphlet, were elaborated by Pufendorf in three official war histories, *Commentarii de rebus Svecicis ab expeditione Gustavi Adolphi in Germaniam, De rebus gestis Friderici Wilhelmi,* and *De rebus a Carolo Gustavo gestis.* However, neither Pufendorf nor any other contemporary ever used the term 'Thirty Years War'. The Italian Galeazzo Gualdo Priorato speaks of 'guerre di Ferdinando II e III e del re Filippo IV di Spagna contro Gustavo Adolfo . . . e Luigi XIII' (1640 and later editions); the Venetian J. Riccius, of the 'bella Germanica' (1649). The references by the duke of Württemberg to the 'twenty years war' (1655) and the 'thirty years war' (1666), and by the Elector of Bavaria to the 'thirty years war' (1659) occur in these rulers' dealings with their Estates. They used these round figures in order to put the blame for their financial demands on the long war instead of, more accurately, on their extravagant princely policy.

Pufendorf's theses were promoted by the 'Great Elector' of Brandenburg, a master of political propaganda. He, who sold himself without any scruples successively or almost simultaneously to Sweden, Poland, Denmark, the Netherlands, the Emperor, and France, liked to pose as an 'honest German' and to identify the interests of the Hohenzollern dynasty with those of Germany. The dark picture which he painted of the war years was meant to highlight the magnitude of his political, economic and cultural successes. At the same time he wished to divert attention away from the abandonment of the peasantry to the tender mercies of the Junkers, the brutal suppression of the Estates in Brandenburg, Cleves-Mark and Prussia and of the age-old liberties of the city of Magdeburg, the oppressive taxation of the townspeople and the tax exemption of the Junkers, and the inordinate expenses for the standing army.

This interpretation of the war and of the role of the Great Elector as the champion of the Protestant religion and of the 'German liberties' against Habsburg oppression and foreign aggression was later taken up by Frederick the Great in his *Mémoires pour servir à l'histoire de la maison de Brandebourg* (1751). Here Frederick contrasts 'the ambition of the house of Austria' with 'the high-minded German princes' fight for freedom'; when 'the Thirty Years War like a mountain torrent had devastated the whole of northern Germany', Frederick William found on his accession a 'hopeless situation' which he redressed by 'repopulating his country and transforming marshes into meadows, deserts into villages, ruins into towns'.

Pufendorf and Frederick the Great were read by academics, diplomatists and administrators. The middle classes of Germany were influenced and captured by two of the most popular authors, Friedrich Schiller and Gustav Freytag, who imprinted their picture of the Thirty Years War upon millions whom no learned dissertation ever reached.

Friedrich Schiller (1759–1805), playwright, poet, philosopher, novelist, wrote two historical works which, owing to his creative imagination and brilliant presentation, represent the acme of historical writing of the pre-critical period. They were his 'History of the secession of the Netherlands' (1788) and his 'History of the Thirty Years War' (1791). Schiller regarded history as 'an inexhaustible magazine for his poetic inspiration' as well as a treasure-house of examples of high virtues and pernicious vices to elevate or warn posterity. He achieved this aim even more emphatically in his dramatic trilogy 'Wallenstein' (1799), the greatest historical play in the German language. While Schiller's psychological interpretation of Wallenstein has not been surpassed by any later writer – historian or poet – the play has also perpetuated many features of the myth evoked by the term 'Thirty Years War', as there can be very few Germans who have not read Schiller's play at school or seen it on the stage.

Schiller's sources were limited entirely to the histories printed in the seventeenth and eighteenth centuries, mostly partisan writings of the Protestant side. Gustav Freytag made available to the reading public a different type of material. Freytag (1816–95), literary historian, journalist, playwright and novelist, exerted considerable influence upon the aesthetic, political and historical tenets of the national-liberal Protestant bourgeoisie of the second half of the nineteenth century. His *Pictures from the German Past* (1859–62, with innumerable reprints) popularized the new branch of 'cultural history'. Freytag excluded political and constitutional history and concentrated on the lives of peasant, citizen, nobleman, priest, housewife and so on. He based his narrative on private correspondence, memoirs, diaries, autobiographies, broadsheets, newspapers and similar sources which historians had largely neglected up to then. In the chapters dealing with the Thirty Years War, Freytag selected such episodes which showed in the most unfavourable light the predecessors of those powers which stood, or were believed to stand, in the way of the nascent Hohenzollern empire: the blighting effect of the Roman Catholic counter-reformation, the selfishness of the princes, the un-German attitude of the house of Habsburg, the anti-German aggressiveness of the French, Poles and Spaniards. With journalistic skill and poetic licence Freytag darkened or lightened the colours, already amply provided by his well-chosen contemporary witnesses, to suit his preconceptions of the 'unparalleled destruction' of the Thirty Years War. The fact that they were actually contemporaries of the events they described impressed Freytag's readers to such an extent that they overlooked the one-sidedness of the selection and the more than liberal use Freytag made in expanding and interpreting this selected material.

In truth, the sources which Freytag and many of his followers used – chronicles, annals, diaries, letters – chiefly show the events of the war as experienced by those who lost most. For the compilers of town chronicles, parish registers, family albums and personal diaries all belonged to the same class of educated, professional men – clerks, priests, officials, lawyers – who were hit hardest by the vicissitudes of the times. Whenever a place was sacked by the enemy, it was the ministers of religion whose persons and property were always the easiest targets. They could not deny the custody of tithe and collection money and of chalices, candlesticks and other valuables. Vicarage, church and monastery were therefore the first objects of any raider, with the additional advantage that the spoliation of papists or heretics would certainly ease the conscience, if any, of protestant or catholic pillagers. Whatever may have befallen the citizens of a town and the peasants of a village, the men who wrote the town chronicles, the monastic annals, the parish registers, were those who had to tell a tale of personal grievance and personal loss; and it is not surprising that their unfortunate personal experiences should have coloured the whole account.

A revision of the Schiller–Freytag picture began towards the end of the nineteenth century. It was economic historians who, by first drawing attention to the hard, material facts underlying political events, destroyed the legend of the pre-ponderantly religious character of the Thirty Years War. However, as these writers dealt of necessity with the unattractive material of import and export returns, production figures, vital statistics and the like, the results of their researches did not attract general attention and did nothing to upset the accepted myth.

It needed, as has been hinted, the shock of two world wars to put the Thirty Years War in its place, to deprive it of the alleged singularity of its horrors and, above all, to destroy its purely German aspect and see it in its European setting.

### The Religious Issues

The label of a 'war of religion' between Roman Catholics and Protestants has been attached to the 'Thirty Years War' by German writers whose philosophy of history was determined successively by the rationalism of the eighteenth, the liberalism of the nineteenth and the agnosticism of the twentieth century. They wrote in an intellectual atmosphere in which religion, philosophy, politics, science, economics and other spheres of human thought and action had become separate entities, divided from one another in almost watertight compartments. These historians therefore completely failed to understand the mentality of sixteenth- and seventeenth-century man. For down to the middle of the seventeenth century members of every community considered life in all its aspects as one integrated whole. There was no division between their religious convictions, their political aspirations, their economic theory and practice: all of them flowed from the concept of human life as one undivided and indivisible universe.

It is therefore quite irrelevant to measure the relative importance of religious considerations against the promptings of statecraft, economic acquisitiveness or even personal aggrandisement, that may have decided the attitude of the statesmen of the period, for none of them would have found himself torn between choices of this kind. Constant use was made in their public utterances of dogmatic arguments derived from the decrees of the council of Trent, the Augsburg confession or the Heidelberg catechism. But what to later ages appeared as merely doctrinal controversies comprised for the seventeenth century debater the whole essence of life.

This complete identification of secular and spiritual issues also explains the rigour with which the various denominations confronted one another. The idea of religious toleration would have appeared not only blasphemous, but contrary to common sense. What actually divided the parties even in the strictly religious sphere (taking it in its modern sense), was less points of creed – which anyway were intelligible only to a handful of academic theologians – but opinions concerning the institution of the visible church. The jurisdiction of the bishop of Rome, the secular power of the episcopate, the usufruct of ecclesiastical property – in fact, the relationship between church and state – these were the problems that agitated the chancelleries and, to some extent, public opinion.

Examination of a few examples of 'religious' attitudes towards the events of the 'Thirty Years War' makes it perfectly clear that it is anachronistic and unprofitable to isolate 'religion' as a determining factor.

Both branches of the house of Habsburg, it is true, represented the life-forces and the aggressive spirit of the church of Rome, as reformed by the council of Trent. But to the Spaniard this crusading zeal was also inseparable from the imperialist expansionism of overseas colonization: a combination epitomized in the first book printed in America which propagated 'Christian doctrine' together with the 'Castilian language'. In Spain itself, adherence to the Roman church meant to the Spanish monarchs the disposal of the vast patronage and wealth of the great orders of chivalry, and close control of the Inquisition whose efficient organization guaranteed the internal security of the state, since heresy and civil disobedience were regarded – and rightly so, in the prevailing spirit of the age – as indistinguishable. Hence the revolt of the Netherlanders imperilled the political coherence of the Empire as much as the Catholic religion; its suppression, from the Spanish point of view, lay in the political interest of the monarchy and the fiscal needs of the treasury as well as in the commandments of the church of God.

A similar blend of motives can be observed in the attitude of the Vienna court towards the Austrian and Bohemian Protestants. Here the dynasty which aimed at creating a centralized and absolutist monarchy, was confronted by nobles who wanted to uphold privileges and strengthen the semi-independence of the various crown-lands where their privileged position was securely entrenched. The victorious Estates would have turned the Habsburg lands into a confederation of Protestant aristocracies; the victorious Emperor welded his possessions into a uniform monarchy, in which loyalty to the Habsburg dynasty and the Roman church was the uniting bond.

In Sweden, the Lutheran establishment was the strongest bulwark of the Vasa dynasty against the claims to the Swedish throne made by their Catholic branch in Poland. Sweden's foreign trade necessitated good relations with the Protestant Hanse towns, the Netherlands and Britain, while Sweden's leading export commodity, copper, had to be protected against the competition of the Tirolese and Hungarian mines which were in Habsburg hands.

Thus, the struggle for the *dominium maris Baltici* set Sweden in opposition to Lutheran Denmark, Catholic Poland and Orthodox Russia. The occupation of the Hartz mines by the imperialists in 1624 endangered the Swedish copper market, and the maritime schemes entertained by Wallenstein and Spain in 1628 threatened Sweden's commercial interests overseas – Gustavus countered these dangers from the Catholic Habsburgs by allying himself with Catholic France.

Likewise, Maximilian of Bavaria, the head of the Catholic League, fought the Lutheran imperial cities of Swabia and Franconia, the Calvinist Palatinate and Netherlands, Lutheran Sweden and finally turned against the Catholic Emperor and Spain. In rarely interrupted co-operation with the Pope, Lutheran Saxony and Catholic France he achieved his main aims: the supersession of his Palatine cousin, the removal of the Spaniards from the Empire and the reduction of the dominant position of the Habsburg Emperor.

Considerations like these leave aside the question of personal faith; this is a matter which must be left to a higher judgment. Humanly speaking, there is no reason to doubt the absolute sincerity with which the champions of the opposing camps, as well as the mass of their humble followers, believed in the truth of their creed. Ferdinand II and Ferdinand III, Maximilian of Bavaria, Tilly, Richelieu and Mazarin were faithful sons of the Roman church; Gustavus Adolphus, Bernard of Weimar, the Electors of Saxony, Brandenburg and the Palatinate, the landgravine of Hesse and the Bohemian nobles were firm Protestants. The Swedish peasants who served under Gustavus fought for the pure gospel, and Tilly's men were fired by an equal zeal for the Holy Virgin; the ones knew nothing of the French subsidies on which they subsisted, the others had no stake in the naked power politics of the Wittelsbachs. Some doubt can be entertained as to the religious aspects of certain conversions. The support which Wolfgang William received from the Catholic League and John Sigismund from the Protestant Union, or the rapid promotion of Pappenheim, Feuquières and Trauttmansdorff after their conversion may at least not have impeded the change of their professed beliefs.

Wallenstein is the one personality whose religious convictions, if any, elude definition. Born into the community of the Bohemian Brethren, he had a Protestant education at school and university. At the age of twenty he was converted to Rome by a Jesuit, who paved his way to the Habsburg court and obtained for him the hand of an elderly widow, the richest heiress of Moravia. Thereafter his religious zeal cooled noticeably and Christian beliefs were increasingly supplanted by the tenets of astrology. His complete unconcern with denominational distinctions made him suspect to Catholics and Protestants alike. His finances were managed by a Calvinist Dutchman; his officer corps was permeated by foreign Protestants and nominal Catholics, amongst whom forcibly converted Bohemians were conspicuous. His indifference can hardly be called genuine toleration; more likely, Wallenstein lacked any religious sentiment.

The emergence of France as the political and cultural leader of Europe was due largely to the fact that the French statesmen of the period – the Protestants Henry IV and Sully, and the Catholics Richelieu and Mazarin – deliberately severed the traditional bond of religion and politics and made the novel concept of *raison d'état* their guiding principle. The exclusion of religious standards enabled France to destroy Protestantism in France and to rescue Protestantism in Germany and the Netherlands, to secure religious and political uniformity at home and to perpetuate the split of western Christendom. Henceforth religious beliefs, orthodox or heretical, were increasingly confined to the sphere of personal conviction and individual choice, whereas public affairs were directed by a *raison d'état* which no longer needed and used supernatural arguments for the pursuit of worldly ends.

## Military Aspects

The raising, training and employment of armies in the first half of the seventeenth century was in essence a large-scale, private-enterprise industry. Both the officers and the men regarded military service as a means of making money and furthering their private interests. The captains, colonels and generals recruited their men from their own resources. Love of adventure, hope of advancement, dissatisfaction or distress were the motives which induced men to flock to the standards raised by solvent entrepreneurs and to sell themselves to the highest bidder. Political, national, religious issues played no part with the common soldier, and very little with the majority of the officers. There was therefore no stigma attached to the soldiers changing sides. The career of Hans Georg von Arnim may serve as an illustration. By birth a vassal of the Elector of Brandenburg, he fought under Gustavus Adolphus against the Poles, joined the Poles in their war with the Turks, entered the imperial army under Wallenstein, obtained an independent command in Poland, became generalissimo of the Saxon army, was offered, but declined, a French commission, and died as imperial and Saxon lieutenant-general while preparing a campaign against the French and Swedes. Instead of being despised as a turncoat, the general and politician Arnim was trusted by friend and foe alike, with the exception of Oxenstierna who once had him arrested and taken as prisoner to Stockholm, whence he made a spectacular escape.

The only soldiers who never wavered in their adherence to the party they had chosen were the English, Scottish and Irish volunteers. The former, opponents of the Stewarts' neutralist foreign policy in England and their episcopalian church policy in Scotland, served under the Bohemian, Danish and Swedish colours; the latter, opponents of the English ascendancy in church and state promoted by the Stewarts in Ireland, were to be found in the Emperor's camp.

The only army which can be described as a national army was the Swedish army which Gustavus Adolphus led into Germany; but this was soon diluted – especially after the fearful losses in the positional warfare near Nürnberg – and the 'Swedish' armies of Bernard, Banér, Torstenson and Königsmark were as international as those of any other belligerent. However, the modern concept of loyalty to the supreme war-lord was first effective in the multi-racial imperial army – the Italian Piccolomini, the Croat Isolani, the Tirolese Gallas, the Luxemburger Aldringen, the Irish Butler – they and nearly every other general and colonel of Wallenstein's kept faith with the Emperor to whom they had sworn fealty rather than their generalissimo from whom they received their pay. These soldiers of fortune realized that in the long run the Emperor – as, later, the king of France – could and did offer them greater security, including titles and other honours, lucrative posts in the administrative and diplomatic services, and the seeming permanence of princely landed estates.

The financial basis of warfare – in other words, the lack of ready cash and the absence of a defence budget – determined the small size of the armies as well as the irregularity of their employment. The proposed establishment and the actual strength of the forces can rarely be assessed with any degree of accuracy. The Catholic League had an effective strength of about 15,000 men, the same number as Gustavus Adolphus put into the field. Wallenstein's first army consisted of 15,000 foot and 6,000 horse. Bernard of Weimar received French subsidies for 18,000 men – Richelieu had originally bargained only for 14,000. Condé's army in 1645, the strongest French contingent employed in Germany, numbered 12,000 men. These figures have only approximate value. The belligerents themselves had no accurate knowledge of either the nominal or the effective strength of their own armies. They probably did not even want to know and preferred juggling with more or less imaginary figures. It is characteristic that during the negotiations about the 'satisfaction' of the Swedish army in 1648, the representatives of the army claimed payment for 125,000 officers and men, whereas the Protestant Estates arrived at 75,000 – both figures based on the same number of regiments. In fact, the terms of regiment, squadron, standard etc. are quite meaningless in themselves. For instance in the battle of Breitenfeld the 15,000 men of the League were organized in 10 regiments, the 15,000 imperialists in 28 regiments; the inflated latter figure is due entirely to Wallenstein's ambition to put as many 'colonels' as possible under obligation to himself.

The need to bring about a decision while the money lasted and the troops could be considered willing to serve, made it almost impossible to carry into effect any strategic conceptions, as we nowadays understand the term. Concerted planning nearly always failed, and the majority of the campaigns were little more than large-scale raids with limited tactical objectives; moreover they always petered out when the immediate aim had been, or had failed to be, achieved. Sound and promising operations could often not be carried out because the troops went on strike, or openly mutinied, when their pay was in arrears or did not come up to their demands. For the same reason the enforcement of strict discipline was often impossible and licentious behaviour of the dissatisfied soldiery had to be tolerated. On the other hand, there was a recognized body of rules of war which was fairly well observed by all parties. The treatment of prisoners of war was lenient – the common soldier was offered service with his captors; officers were easily exchanged or discharged on parole. The sack of Magdeburg, often pilloried as a fiendish outrage (just as afterwards the 'massacre' of Drogheda), was in reality entirely within the accepted custom – after the third and final summons for surrender had been refused, the victorious assault troops were entitled to a three-day pillage.

On the whole, the science of logistics was little developed. Many of the complaints about the burden which the provisioning and quartering of troops imposed upon a rural district or a town reflect lack of foresight and organization rather than deliberate malice and cruelty. The very efficiency with which Wallenstein solved logistic problems added to the resentment of the princes and great landowners against him. Methodical requisitioning by his quartermasters was felt more irksome and was more bitterly resented than the indiscriminate pillaging by a band of marauders which could be shrugged off as a natural phenomenon.

Consideration for the well-being and comfort of officers and men was responsible for the suspension of military activities during the winter months, almost the equivalent of furlough in a modern army. Hence the successes of the Swedish generals who again and again surprised their opponents by disregarding the traditional 'close season' – the battles of Lützen (1632), Breitenfeld (1642) and Jankov (1645), the conquest of Regensburg (1633) and Breisach (1638) took place when the imperial generals least expected.

The short duration of the campaigning seasons also disposes of the legend of the ruinous effects of 'the' war upon German economic and cultural life. It was only the districts of primary strategic importance which had to bear the brunt of successive invasions or prolonged occupation in the seventeenth century, as they have been the focal points of every warlike operation in central Europe from Roman times to the Second World War:

the Rhine crossings of Breisach and Wesel; the plains of Brabant and Leipzig; the passes across the Thuringian and Black Forests; and the roads leading to Regensburg, Prague and Vienna. Other tracts of Germany were either not at all affected as, for example, Lower Bavaria, Tirol, Oldenburg, or only for a few weeks during the 'thirty' years. The majority of towns (including Hamburg, Lübeck, Bremen, Danzig and Stralsund) never saw an enemy inside their walls. Magdeburg, the one city suffering almost complete destruction, can be cited with equal justification as an example of successful and speedy reconstruction. Otto von Guericke, town-councillor, structural engineer and physicist, was commissioned by the Swedish resident to draw up a comprehensive plan for the rebuilding of the city; by 10 April 1632 he had accomplished this task. His plan (now in the Swedish state archives) is as bold and farsighted as those submitted by Wren or Holford for post-1666 and post-1945 London – and like them was scrapped in favour of more humdrum designs. Nevertheless, by 1680 the town had been completely rebuilt, with Guericke, from 1646 a burgomaster, as the driving force.

## Economic Aspects

In dealing with the effects of the 'Thirty Years War' upon the economic life of Germany, we are confronted with exceptional difficulties. To begin with, the term 'Germany' is itself open to various interpretations during the half-century under discussion. One can surely leave out of consideration the Italian relics of the Holy Roman Empire, such as Savoy, Milan, Parma, Modena, Genoa, Tuscany. On the other hand, the United Provinces and the Swiss Confederation until 1648, the Spanish Netherlands, Lorraine and Franche-Comté even longer, were nominal members of the empire, whereas Prussia, Schleswig and Upper Hungary lay outside its frontiers. In the three last-named provinces a considerable part, perhaps the majority, of the population were of German stock; in Bohemia, Moravia, Upper Silesia, Carniola, and the bishopric of Trent – all undoubtedly parts of the Empire – the Germans were a minority. It is clear that the inclusion or exclusion of any of these countries will intrinsically influence the image of seventeenth-century Germany.

The second point that makes virtually impossible any clear-cut notion of the conditions in which the people of this elusive

'Germany' lived, is the absence of comprehensive contemporary statistical data relating to population, production, finances. There are, to be sure, occasional surveys of the recruitment of militiamen, of the number of houses burnt down or else made uninhabitable by enemy action, the contributions levied in cash or kind, the victims of an epidemic or a massacre – but all such figures are to be treated with caution and suspicion. Almost without exception, enumerations of this kind were made for some special purpose – usually in order to show that the town or district was incapable of furnishing a required number of men or beasts, of supplying corn or timber, of paying ordinary or extraordinary taxes. In consequence, productivity and solvency were always as much underrated as losses and hardships were exaggerated. Moreover, all these accounts were rendered for certain small districts only. The only inquiry of this kind that covered a whole principality is that ordered in 1652 by the government of Württemberg; but the figures supplied – including the 'war damages' of precisely 118,742,864 guilders – are open to serious doubt. The most plausible explanation: the Württemberg Estates were the most powerful as well as the most vocal institution of their kind in the whole of Germany; they would certainly not let pass an occasion for the most extravagant claims on the purse of their duke! It is therefore easy to see that any generalization will only multiply the errors inherent in the original figures.

A feature common to annalists and journalists of all times is a preference for a singular startling event, to the exclusion of every-day occurences not deemed worth mentioning. The death from the plague of half a dozen local worthies will naturally attract the chronicler's attention more than the unspectacular birth of a hundred children during the same period; and the fleeting appearance of a turbulent squadron of Croat horsemen in a Westphalian village must have left a deeper impression than the caravans of carters who from time immemorial had passed by on their way from Cologne to Bremen.

Instead of offering an overall picture, it is therefore necessary to assemble a mosaic of details. Their presentation is entirely dependent on the unco-ordinated state of research made here and there and consequently of no validity for other parts of the country, much less for Germany as a whole.

*Population.* Historical demography must be based on the detailed study of small social and geographical units; nation-wide estimates are almost useless before the first real censuses were undertaken in the eighteenth century. Estimates of population figures were, until quite recently, hampered by the fact that historians were on the whole unfamiliar with statistical and demographic methods, while statisticians and demographers lacked interest in, or knowledge of, historical questions or method. Historians have relied too much on the guesswork, often tendentious, of chroniclers and pamphleteers, or at most on the parish registers of deaths. Hence the figures, readily accepted, of a decline of the population during the war by one-third, one-half or even two-thirds. Two typical examples – there were 6,009 burials in the city of Nijmegen in 1635–36; therefore, the historian who has assembled these figures naïvely concludes that the number of inhabitants fell from 15,000 to 9,000. The death-roll in Olomouc in Moravia for the year 1624 is given as 14,000 – which would amount to 100 per cent. or more of the total population. An investigation of the parish registers of marriages and births would rectify this miscalculation, for the huge birth-rate of the time supplies almost exactly that third or half by which the population is said to have been reduced.

In considering the causes of death, we can omit the losses sustained on the battlefield. In view of the smallness of the contending armies the numbers of killed were proportionally insignificant. The greatest and most dreaded killers were epidemics, chiefly typhoid, the plague and venereal diseases; they were spread by soldiers, refugees and rats, and rendered more deadly by the lack of hygiene and the incompetence of doctors.

An almost unique calculation of the effect of the pestilence or plague (the generic terms used for any kind of epidemic) on the population exists for the town of Kalkar near Wesel: from 1473 to 1585 the accounts have been preserved for every coffin manufactured, with exact lists of the dead. There were during this century about a dozen major outbreaks of 'the death', but the population of Kalkar rose from about 2,400 to 4,000 persons. There is no reason to doubt that similar figures, if they were available, would apply to the next century as well. Taking count of statistics, admittedly less detailed, compiled for other towns, it can be asserted that the mortality rate never surpassed 12 per cent. and probably averaged about 6 to 8 per cent.

A model investigation, literally house by house, of the small town of Uelzen in Lower Saxony has clarified the effect upon different professions of the plague (in its proper medical sense). As the plague is communicated by brown rats infected by fleas, the habits of the rats largely determine the degree of danger to human beings. Bakers, butchers and weavers are the most susceptible, as the rats find food and warmth in their houses, whereas smiths and coopers are comparatively immune because rats are very sensitive to noise. This observation also disposes of a common fallacy: during a particularly severe plague in Hamburg 35 per cent. of the bakers and 45 per cent. of the butchers died. But these two professions are most exposed to the infestation by rats, as demonstrated in Uelzen; it is therefore inadmissible to conclude that between one-third and one-half of the Hamburg population was carried off, as has been asserted.

There are plenty of other explanations for the temporary or permanent decline of population, such as the evacuation from the open country into walled towns, for which the evacuation of townspeople to the country during the Second World War provides a parallel in reverse: in both cases the evacuees went to places of greater safety. The population of Kiel, Lübeck and Hamburg was swollen by the influx of the landed gentry and their retainers from Holstein. Neutral Basel in 1638 harboured 7,600 South-German refugees in addition to its 20,000 citizens. Hanover owed its rise in population and prosperity to the fact that Duke George chose it as his capital in 1636, when the castles of Calenberg and Neustadt had proved their unsuitability as seats of government by falling easy preys to Tilly's assaults.

The temporary dislocation of populations can be seen in five Thuringian rural districts: numbers declined between 1631 and 1649 by as much as 66 per cent. or even 87 per cent. and rose in the following decade from 78 per cent. to 125 per cent. – in other words, the evacuees had returned. Similarly, during the decade of 1640–50 the Altmark, west of Magdeburg, lost thousands of fugitives to Hamburg, Holstein, Saxony and Poland and at the same time gained thousands of refugees from Bremen, Friesland and Holstein.

Sometimes the migration was due to reasons of economic betterment: young men flocked from the agrarian village to the industrial town, far-sighted business men went from the economically declining to the economically rising city. Some of the wealthiest men of Cologne moved to Frankfurt; the Protestant Walloons and the Merchants Adventurers, who from the 1580s had made little Stade a leading emporium, went to Hamburg after 1612, with the result that neither Cologne nor Stade ever recovered their former prosperity. A modern example helps to understand this fluctuation – the decrease of the London population by 2 million between 1938 and 1946 indicates that a large number of Londoners were temporarily evacuated, or had permanently moved into outer suburbia: it does not mean that 2 million Londoners perished in the war.

Some places even profited directly by the wars. To the manufacturers of rifles and other small arms in the Westphalian town of Essen the continuous demand for their wares by all parties provided full employment as well as security. The Spanish garrison in Aachen and the Swedish garrison in Minden saw to it, in their own interest, that these towns came through the war undamaged.

For the Spanish Netherlands, perhaps the most war-scarred part of the Empire and western Europe, some population figures have been compiled which leave the impression that none of the campaigns fought on its soil between the arrival of Alba and the departure of Marlborough had any appreciable effect on the steady growth of its towns. Antwerp increased from 42,000 inhabitants in 1589 to 67,000 in 1699; Louvain had 10,000 in 1600 and 13,000 in 1709; Ghent 31,000 in 1606–15 and 52,000 in 1686–95. No comparable figures are available for the rural districts, so that it is impossible to say what proportion of this growth is due to natural increase and what to immigration from the countryside – a lack of information which here as elsewhere invalidates all hasty assumptions.

To sum up, the most plausible explanation of the indubitable depletion of certain parts of Germany as well as the equally ascertainable increase of other parts is to be found in an extensive internal migration and redistribution of population. Its net result at the end of our period was a small increase of the total population, such as is characteristic of every predominantly agricultural society. If the elasticity of the term 'Germany' is borne in mind, one may postulate a total population of about 15 to 17 million in 1600 and about 16 to 18 million in 1650.

*Industry, Trade and Agriculture.* Turning to German economy proper, we are again faced with the lack of any overall statistics and have to build up the general picture out of more or less reliable details. The simple addition or multiplication of results obtained here and there is quite inadmissible as a means of describing the German economy as a whole.

From the middle of the thirteenth century the towns were the undisputed masters of German economic life. Even agriculture, if not brought under the direct control of city financiers, was at least completely dependent upon the town markets for home consumption and upon the shipping facilities provided by the towns for export overseas. It is therefore the urban economy which above all has to be studied.

The traditional assumption of a general decline of the German cities during the seventeenth century is based on a confusion of their political and their economic status. There can, of course, be no doubt that the political role of the cities was finished. The maintenance of a precarious neutrality was the most that could still be used as a political weapon, and that only by a few of the biggest towns – Danzig, Lübeck, Hamburg, Frankfurt, Nürnberg. Many decades before the outbreak of the 'Thirty Years War' political power had come to rest with the half-dozen leading princes.

However, the political insignificance of the cities was by no means paralleled by their economic downfall. What happened throughout the seventeenth century was a reorientation of industry, trade and commerce. The decay or extinction of an old-established industry must always seem like the end of the world to those unfortunates who cannot or will not accommodate themselves to changed circumstances. The Spanish Netherlands, still part of the Empire, offers a telling example of economic myths attributed to the Thirty- or, in this case, the Eighty-Years War. The country was affected by every campaign fought by Spaniards, Dutch, French and English; the woollen industry, since the early middle ages the basis of Flemish prosperity, was moribund; the port of Bruges, once the centre of western European trade, had silted up and become useless; the mouth of the river Scheldt was in the hands of the Dutch enemy who thereby controlled the sea passage to and from Antwerp. In short, Belgian historians have characterized the seventeenth century as 'the century of misery' (*le siècle de malheur*), and Belgian public opinion has accepted this description. An unemotional investiga-

tion into what actually happened in this period presents a different picture. True, the woollen industry went downhill as the
Dutch, French and above all the English captured the former
Flemish markets and, even more important, European fashion
changed from the heavy woollen fabrics to lighter materials, such
as serge and linen. But this challenge was taken up. In Liège and
Herve a flourishing serge industry grew up, Verviers created its
linen industry, and in Flanders far-sighted producers went over
to the manufacture of linen. Elsewhere large-scale coal-mining
was established, but above all, luxury articles fashioned in Belgian
shops were marketed all over Europe: lace-work, tapestry, glass-
cutting, diamond-cutting and, not least, printing, for the house
of Plantin in Antwerp was throughout the Eighty Years War
the leading publisher-printer in Catholic Europe. A network of
canals helped the Antwerp skippers to maintain, perhaps to
increase, the seaborne traffic despite the war-time closure of the
Scheldt by the Dutch, not to mention Antwerp's flourishing and
hardly interrupted 'enemy trade' with the Dutch. In 1644–49
the English agriculturist Sir Richard Weston visited Flanders
and Brabant and commented favourably on the intensive cultiva-
tion of the country and the manifest wealth of the farmers. In
fact, the devastations caused by military actions were far outweighed by the benefits which the quietly efficient rule of the
archducal couple Albert and Isabel (1596–1633) and the
Cardinal-Infant Ferdinand (1633–41) bestowed upon the country.
   A similar shift can be noted in the south German town of
Augsburg. Once, its bankers and traders had successfully dabbled
in international politics: Maximilian I had delighted in the nick-
name of 'burgomaster of Augsburg'; the colossal bribes furnished
by the banking house of Fugger had secured the election as
Emperor of Charles V; the house of Welser had acquired from
the Spanish crown huge concessions in the colony of 'Little
Venice', Venezuela. But the close connexion with the Austrian
and Spanish Habsburgs entailed the ruin of the Welsers. The
revocation of the privileges in Venezuela and the successive
bankruptcies of the Spanish crown eventually, in 1614, brought
about the spectacular ruin of the firm. The Fuggers too, for a
hundred and fifty years the richest German industrialists, im-
porters and exporters, and bankers, suffered great losses through
their financial ties with the Emperor and Spain. It is significant
that the handwritten 'Fugger newsletters' which supplied the

chanceries and business houses of Europe with political and economic intelligence ceased in 1605. However, the ruin of the big bankers and industrialists did not finish Augsburg. The replanning and rebuilding of the town – public and private buildings alike – by the city architect Elias Holl from 1590 to 1630 made 'golden Augsburg' the most beautiful renaissance town north of the Alps. Augsburg weavers proved their unbroken vitality by changing over to cotton from fustian, the original backbone of Augsburg's industry and now going out of fashion; in calico-printing Augsburg achieved a near-monopoly in seventeenth- and eighteenth-century continental Europe.

The imperial city of Nürnberg weathered the war years undamaged. The few weeks in 1632 when Gustavus Adolphus and his staff made Nürnberg their headquarters was the only time when soldiers other than the city guard were inside the walls. The foundation of the 'Banco Publico' during the inflationary period (1621) maintained Nürnberg's reputation for financial honesty. The fame of Nürnberg's art and craft products increased; musical instruments, watches, and children's toys became profitable export goods. The city's college at Altdorf, founded in 1580, where Wallenstein had been a student, was raised to university status in 1623. The publishing firm of Endter was the biggest printing establishment in the Empire.

The confederation of Lübeck, Hamburg and Bremen in 1630 signified the virtual end of the Hanseatic League which at times had comprised a hundred cities or more. Before that, the Hanse had lost its privileged position in England, Russia, Sweden and the Netherlands; the Dutch and the English were invading the Baltic, for centuries the monopolistic market of the Hanse merchants. But neither the political decline of the Hanse nor the 'Thirty Years War' had an adverse effect upon the commercial standing of the maritime towns. Until about 1645 their trade showed an upward trend. Military events did not affect Hamburg and Lübeck. What happened to these two towns was a complete reversal of their former position. Lübeck, for centuries the head of the Hanse, now took second place after Hamburg and was gradually surpassed also by Bremen, both of which had the advantage of a geographical position nearer to the Atlantic sea-routes. The establishment in 1619, of the big clearing bank, on the model of the Amsterdam bank, secured for Hamburg a leading role in international finance – the Hamburg 'Mark

Banco' was the most stable currency until the £ sterling took its place about 1800.

Hamburg emerged from the 'Thirty Years' War' as the wealthiest German city. In 1618 it had achieved its age-old ambition and been recognized by the supreme tribunal of the Empire as a free imperial city. Between 1616 and 1625 a Dutch engineer had redesigned its fortifications which made Hamburg an impregnable fortress. During all the wars of the seventeenth and eighteenth centuries the Hamburg senate observed a strict neutrality, which assured the uninterrupted growth of Hamburg's shipping and trade. This neutrality was even welcomed by the belligerents as it left open to them a place where agents and go-betweens could meet; at some time Charles I and Parliament were represented by rival envoys. The Swedes established a permanent residency in Hamburg as early as 1620. From 1624 their agent was Johann Adler Salvius who remained there until his death in 1652, only absent in Osnabrück during the final stages of the peace congress. He was joined in 1635 by a French envoy; from 1637 to 1643 this was the Comte d'Avaux, later the leading French diplomatist in Münster. Both agents used Hamburg as a basis for buying up war material and enlisting soldiers; Adler Salvius can in fact be said to have run the greater part of Sweden's war economy from Hamburg. Hamburg was also the place where Adler Salvius and d'Avaux in 1638 and 1641 signed the agreements renewing the Franco–Swedish alliance, and where, on Christmas Day 1641, they and the Emperor's envoy concluded the 'preliminary peace' which formed the starting point of the negotiations in Münster and Osnabrück. A special attraction of Hamburg was the ease with which the Hamburg Bank and individual merchant-bankers could transact exchange business on a vast international scale. All the French subsidies to Sweden and the German princes, all the expenses for purchasing stores and hiring soldiers, all the purchases and sales transacted in Amsterdam – amounting to millions of talers year by year – went through Hamburg banking accounts; and burgomaster Moller who openly accepted a French pension cannot have been the only Hamburger to snap up his share of this golden shower.

The shipping and customs records of Danzig and Hamburg, the leading Baltic and North Sea ports, reveal the effect of war and peace upon business conditions throughout northern and western Europe. Apart from the years of the Swedish blockade of Danzig during the Swedish-Polish war (1626–29) and of the Danish blockade of the Elbe in 1630, the sea-going traffic of both places shows an almost uninterrupted upward trend from about 1620. The temporary elimination of their Dutch rivals after the resumption of the Spanish-Dutch war in 1621 and after the outbreak of the first Anglo-Dutch war in 1652 brought about exceptional booms. But even before and after these unexpected chances both cities profited by the steadily increasing demand of the urban populations and the navies of the Netherlands, England, Spain, Portugal and Italy for the grain, timber, tallow, hemp and pitch which the Baltic, Polish, Bohemian and North-German noblemen produced and shipped through Danzig, Hamburg and other German ports such as Stettin and Bremen. Hamburg also became the chief port of transit for the shipment of metallic and non-metallic ores, such as Hungarian copper and Italian alum, to Amsterdam and Spain, ousting Antwerp from this profitable trade. The quantity and value of Danzig exports in the 1630s and 1640s was reached and surpassed only in the nineteenth century.

The duties paid to the Danish exchequer for the passage through the Sound rose steadily throughout the first half of the seventeenth century and provide a yardstick for the flourishing trade carried to and from Lübeck, Danzig, Königsberg; the actual shipments undoubtedly surpassed those registered. On the other hand, the old Hanseatic towns of Rostock, Stralsund and Wismar were undoubtedly on the decline. But this had begun already about 1600 and was quite unconnected with the 'Thirty Years War'. It was entirely due to the invasion of the Baltic by Dutch and English shipping; the Dutch freighters especially were larger, faster and therefore more economic than the old Hanseatic vessels. Nevertheless, there was no continuous decline and during some periods even a certain improvement. The haphazard survival of statistical material allows only glimpses which can never convey a complete picture. Thus the shipping lists of Wismar begin only in 1636 when the port handled 671 vessels; their number rose to 1,191 in 1639 and thereafter fell to 693 in 1643 and 302 in 1644 – neither the extraordinary rise in 1639 nor the crash five years later can be explained satisfactorily. However, these figures give the lie to the complaint voiced by the town council in 1633 that Wismar's trade was completely ruined. In fact, the virtual annexation of Wismar by Sweden in 1631 conferred upon the port all the advantages of being included in the economy of a great power.

The customs accounts of the Rostock port of Warnemünde show a similar discrepancy of rise and fall which does not fit into any preconceived scheme. On the one hand, the number of vessels entering and leaving Warnemünde was nearly twice as large in 1636/37 as it had been in 1599 (926 against 501), and Rostock's beer export in 1636 was double that of 1586. On the other hand, the sea-borne traffic from Rostock to Denmark–Norway declined catastrophically from 212 vessels employed in 1619 to 61 in 1644. But this was the result of the protectionist policy of Christian IV of Denmark-Norway who deliberately favoured Danish-Norwegian and, to some degree, Dutch shipping against the Hanse towns. This is evident from the collapse of Hanseatic shipping to the Norwegian port of Bergen – it fell from 167 vessels in 1600 to 30 in 1640.

The ledgers of two Stralsund textile merchants give evidence of the almost uninterrupted business dealings during the war years. One of them bought in Hamburg between 1620 and 1649 an annual average of 1,000 metres of expensive English cloth. The second regularly attended the Easter and Michaelmas fairs in Leipzig between 1619 and 1627 – unfortunately we do not know whether he resumed his travels after the siege of 1628 and the Swedish occupation in 1631.

Whereas Wismar profited by its inclusion in the Swedish economic system, the Pomeranian town of Elbing suffered only disadvantages from the Swedish occupation (1626–35). Its expansion and rebuilding as a strong fortress offered no compensation for the loss of its economic prosperity. For the Polish king withdrew the privileges granted to the English Trading Company in Elbing, and the English transferred their business to Danzig, then under Polish suzerainty.

Danzig gained enormously at the expense not only of Elbing but also of the towns of the Polish hinterland. Here the Polish nobility went into business, taking over the profitable export of grain and timber from their estates, and cutting out the urban middlemen, thereby causing the permanent impoverishment of the citizenry, chiefly Germans and Jews. It is a symbol of Danzig's prosperity that the city attracted the best seventeenth-century engraver of medals, Sebastian Dadler, who worked here from 1634 to 1648. Dadler's migrations can indeed be taken as indicative of the places which offered scope and security to a skilled craftsman and artist: a native of Strasbourg, he went successively to Augsburg, Dresden, Danzig and finally Hamburg.

The example of the Polish nobleman replacing the German citizen in the corn and timber trade is perhaps typical of a trend in agriculture elsewhere. Again, we notice a regrouping of ownership and profits, the rise of one section of the population being balanced by the retrogression of another. The depopulation of the countryside and the disappearance of hundreds of villages and thousands of homesteads has always been recognized as a feature of seventeenth century life; and it has usually been ascribed to the 'Thirty Years War'. Now, it cannot be doubted that the open country is more exposed to the ill-effects of this, as of any, war than the towns. No village could withstand a siege as did Stralsund; and numerous villages and country seats were wholly or partly burned down, some more than once. But the villages that disappeared from the map were those which were laid waste by the feudal owners of the big estates, the *Junkers* as they were called in the lands east of the river Elbe. The steady rise of corn prices and the increasing demands of the urban population throughout western Europe from the middle of the sixteenth century taught them that huge profits could be made out of large-scale farming and stock-breeding and the bulk-selling of farm produce and livestock. Long before the first shot of the 'Thirty Years War' was fired, the *Junkers* had begun the wholesale eviction of peasants, the forced acquisition of peasant land and the levelling of peasant dwellings. The wars proved a further source of gain to the big landowners: to the armies of both sides they supplied provisions of cereals and cattle from their fields and pastures and timber from their forests. Count Anton Günther of Oldenburg presented Mansfeld, Tilly, Christian of Denmark, the Emperor, the Swedish, French and Hessian generals and diplomatists with the renowned saddle-horses from his stud-farm, and thus brought his country undamaged and enriched through the wars. No such openings were available to the small farmer. He could not compete with the lord of the manor even if he had any surplus to sell; he and his family were the first victims of marauders – while the neighbouring nobleman had removed himself and his household to the security of a walled town. It was especially in those districts which suffered least from military inroads – Prussia, Pomerania, Mecklenburg, Brandenburg, Schleswig-Holstein – where the once free farmer was reduced to virtual or legal serfdom and the political and economic preponderance of the *Junkers* was firmly established for the next three hundred years. The rustics, evicted from their ancestral lands and left without prospect of a decent livelihood, therefore provided the man-power for the mercenary armies, as later on for the industrial factories.

The two Holstein towns of Glückstadt and Friedrichstadt, founded only a few years before the outbreak of the Danish war, offer good examples of the security of town life, of the possibility of industrial expansion and of the balance of gain and loss as regards the movement of population. Glückstadt was intended to be a maritime rival of Hamburg. It was made the headquarters of Danish companies trading to Africa, Iceland, Norway and the East Indies and withstood unharmed several sieges (1628, 1630, 1643–45). Both towns attracted large numbers of Dutch dissenters (Remonstrants and Mennonites), Lutherans from Augsburg, Socinians from Poland, Roman Catholics from Flanders, Quakers from England and Jews from Portugal, all of whom were granted freedom of worship. These immigrants introduced numerous new manufactures which flourished throughout the seventeenth century.

The Saxon city of Leipzig can be adduced as an outstanding example of how an active and indefatigable population of enterprising tradesmen and hardworking manufacturers overcame the ill-effects of wars, epidemics and mismanagement of public finance. The corrupt city council had run Leipzig into debt and in 1625 had to declare itself bankrupt; the Elector's government placed Leipzig under sequestration from 1627 to 1688. In 1631 Tilly ravaged Leipzig after having burned down its suburbs; in 1632 Wallenstein occupied the town and in 1633 his general Holk shelled it; Banér laid siege to it in 1637, and in 1642 Leipzig had to capitulate to the Swedes who garrisoned it until 1650. The battles of Breitenfeld (1631, 1642) and Lützen (1632) were fought before its gates. In brief, if any town suffered from the direct and indirect consequences of the Thirty Years War, it was Leipzig. In fact, the period of the 'Thirty Years War' saw Leipzig emerge as the leading German trade centre, second only to Hamburg and far outpacing Nürnberg, Cologne and Frankfurt. In these years, the twice-annual Leipzig fairs established themselves as the meeting points of European wholesale and retail merchants. In 1640, three years after the most devastating outbreak of the plague and the siege by Banér, the city council reported that Leipzig businessmen nursed regular trade contacts with Brabant, England, Italy, Poland, the Ukraine, Scandinavia, and Muscovy. By 1650 Leipzig had gained supremacy in two commodities, which remained its specialities until 1933: the import, processing and export of Russian furs, and the production, publishing and distribution of books.

In conclusion it may, therefore, be said that the inflation of the years 1619–23 had destroyed the accumulated gains of the preceding century, or rather, it had effected a thorough transfer of capital and property. Hardly any of the old firms of international repute had survived. They were replaced by successful speculators, army contractors and other *homines novi* who made the most of fresh opportunities. The losses sustained by one individual, one city, one district, were counterbalanced by the gains made elsewhere. On the whole, the national income, productivity and standard of living were higher in 1650 than they had been fifty years earlier. If nevertheless the Germany of 1650 presents a less prosperous all-round picture than the Germany of 1550, this impression is correct if one compares German economic life with that of the Netherlands, France and England. These countries were forging ahead with might and main; Germany could not keep the pace set by them and therefore appears stationary, though it was far from actually declining.

## Cultural Life

The legend of the cultural desolation, intellectual exhaustion and moral degradation of the German people as a result of the 'Thirty Years War' is perhaps easiest to refute.

The disdain and denigration of the German achievement in literature and music, art and architecture, philosophy and science were solely due to the aesthetic standards of nineteenth-century critics. To them the 'baroque' style was anathema, as 'gothic' had been to the arbiters of the eighteenth century; and since the civilization of the seventeenth century was 'baroque', it was condemned out of hand. The revaluation which has taken place during the past forty years or so, makes it unnecessary to defend the writers and artists of the period of the 'Thirty Years

War'. Their place in the history of German civilization is now secure.

In art and architecture, the production of native painters, sculptors and architects was completely outclassed by the work of foreigners. The Viennese and south German courts on the whole preferred Italian masters: in the north, Dutch influence was as strong. The best German painters worked abroad – Flinck in Amsterdam, Lely in London. The Dutch painter Peter Candid, a pupil of Vasari in Rome, was employed by Maximilian of Bavaria; the Dutch sculptor, Adriaen de Vries, by the Emperor Rudolf II and the city of Augsburg.

However, after the mania of building during the prosperous sixteenth century there was little need for replacing the splendid palaces and town halls, churches and patrician houses of the immediate past. It was only newcomers in church and state who gave work to architects and interior decorators: Wallenstein commissioned his palaces in Prague, Jičin and Sagan; his friend Eggenberg, the magnificent castle near Graz. The new religious orders, such as the Carmelites, Barnabites and Servites, outrivalled the older foundations by sumptuous edifices. Lutherans and Calvinists, too, had the will and money to build new churches where required, unimpeded by the din of war.

Most private buildings of the period are insignificant from the artistic and art-historical viewpoint and have therefore failed to gain mention in architectural handbooks, even if they have not been destroyed by fire or been pulled down in favour of later buildings. But there was a great interest in textbooks on urban architecture, no doubt due partly to the continuous migration from the country to the town. Rüdiger Kossmann of Cologne wrote a handbook in 1630, of which revised editions came out in 1644 and 1653; and Josef Furtenbach of Ulm published three very popular books on *Architectura Civilis* (1628), *Recreationis* (1640) and *Privata* (1641) – they must have met a lively demand on the part of designers, builders and customers.

Lyrical poetry reached new heights, surpassed only in the age of Goethe, with the Swabian Georg Rudolf Weckherlin (Milton's predecessor as 'Latin Secretary' under the Commonwealth), the Prussian Simon Dach, the Saxon Paulus Gerhardt, the Rhenish Jesuit, Friedrich von Spee (also famous as an intrepid fighter against the superstition of witchcraft); and above all, the brilliant school of Silesian authors, such as Friedrich von

Logau, Andreas Gryphius, Hofmann von Hofmannswaldau, Angelus Silesius. There is hardly a modern anthology that does not include specimens of their verse. Their head was Martin Opitz, himself a second-rate poet, but immensely important for his ceaseless activities as a translator and especially for his *Buch von der teutschen Poeterey* (1624). This book supplied German poetry with a theoretical basis which was observed for a hundred and fifty years. It was supplemented by the Lower Saxon author Schottel's *Deutsche Sprachkunst* (1641) which standardized German grammar and prose.

Of the German novelists of the period, only one has stood the test of time – and he for the wrong reason. Hans Christoffel von Grimmelshausen's picaresque novel *Der abenteurliche Simplicissimus* (1668) is always mentioned as the chief contemporary witness of the horrors of the Thirty Years War – by people who know the book only from hearsay or have picked out some of the purple-patches. The novel is, in fact, a religious discourse on the vanity of the world and the salvation of the soul, illustrated by the vicissitudes of the hero's life against the background of war and peace – in many respects a wordly 'Pilgrim's Progress'. Far from regarding the 'Thirty Years' War' as an unmitigated evil, Simplicissimus on the whole led a jolly life, troubled only by nagging doubts about the riddle of human existence and the venereal disease which he caught during his stay in Paris.

The mass of contemporary novels, including Grimmelshausen's other writings, have now been forgotten. But it is worth noting that the majority of fictional reading consisted in translations from the Italian, Spanish and French, and has therefore been kept out of the histories of German literature, which also take no notice of the flourishing neo-Latin poets of the time, amongst whom the Jesuit Jacob Balde is one of the greatest by any standards. This is an interesting parallel with the translations, chiefly of English and American books, which swamped the German market after the Second World War – again, not part of German literature proper but certainly to be taken into account when assessing the literary life of the country.

The development of the German stage was favoured by the baroque delight in high-flown histrionics and ostentatious décor. Courts and town councils, universities and schools celebrated every suitable event with fairy masques, heroic tragedies, and coarse comedies. Troups of 'English comedians' gave the German public a first inkling of Shakespeare. The comedies of the Silesian poet Andreas Gryphius show Shakespeare's influence; his *Peter Squentz* is an adaptation of *Midsummer Night's Dream*. One of his tragedies, *Carolus Stuardus*, dealt sympathetically with a topical English subject – just as the English playwright Henry Glapthorne presented the patrons of the London Globe with *The Tragedy of Albertus Wallenstein* (1639). As a thanks-offering after an outbreak of the plague, the little Bavarian village of Oberammergau began in 1634 to produce its famous Passion Play which has preserved into the present the popular aspect of the dramatic art of the baroque. At the other end of the social scale, the court of Dresden launched the German opera and the German ballet: here the court composer Heinrich Schütz, a pupil of Monteverdi, performed in 1627 his opera *Dafne*, for which Martin Opitz wrote the libretto, and a decade later his ballet *Orpheus und Eurydice*. The Dresden example was followed in other protestant courts, whereas the brilliant musical life of Vienna and Munich was dominated exclusively by Italian musicians.

In the field of the natural and political sciences two German scholars even attained international fame, the astronomer Johannes Kepler and the lawyer Johannes Althusius. The Swabian Kepler perfected and completed the cosmological system of Copernicus, though, while in the service successively of the Protestant Estates of Styria and Upper Austria, the Emperor Rudolf II and Wallenstein, he was often forced to waste his genius on the compilation of astrological prognostications. The Westphalian Althusius spent his most fruitful years as professor at the little university of Herborn, later becoming the town clerk of Emden; he was the first to apply the name of 'politics' to what is now known as political science and sociology which he expounded in *Politica methodice digesta*.

All these efforts in the humanities and sciences were encouraged and promoted by a number of literary and scientific societies which attracted the best intellects of the country. The oldest and most influential of them was the Weimar *Fruchtbringende Gesellschaft* (Fructifying Society, founded in 1617), modelled on the Florentine Accademia della Crusca; it was followed by the Hamburg *Teutschgesinnte Genossenschaft* (True-German Society, 1643), the Nürnberg *Pegnitzorden* (Order of the river Pegnitz, 1644) and others. Whereas these societies were chiefly concerned with the improvement of linguistic, literary and critical standards, the Rostock *Naturwissenschaftliche Gesellschaft* (Scientific Society, 1622) was the first learned body expressly constituted for the advancement of the natural sciences.

The wide distribution of reading matter was facilitated by a well-organized book-market and the efficient productivity of some big and many small publishers and printers, and an expanding news-service. The book-fairs of Frankfurt and Leipzig were attracting publishers, booksellers, printers and typefounders from all over Europe. The Frankfurt fair-catalogue was considered so essential a bibliographical aid that a London stationer brought out an English edition (1617–28). The two greatest German publishers, Endter of Nürnberg and Stern of Lüneburg, rivalled in output – though not in quality – the two giants of European publishing, Plantin in Antwerp and Elzevir in Leiden. The house of Stern had customers in places as far afield as Amsterdam, Stockholm, Danzig, Reval and Vilna. Endter brought out the German writings of the great educationalist Jan Amos Komenský, whose *Orbis pictus* can be acclaimed as the first schoolbook designed on the principles of child-psychology; Endter also published Harsdörffer's *Frauenzimmer-Gesprächspiele* (Playful discussions of women, 1644–49), the first periodical directly aimed at a female public.

Frankfurt was also the place chosen by two foreigners for the exercise of the art of copper-engraving: Theodore de Bry, a native of Liège, and his son-in-law Matthäus Merian, of Basel. Merian engraved over 2,000 views of towns for the thirty volumes of *Topographia*, a priceless descriptive and pictorial record of seventeenth-century towns in Germany, France and Italy. It was not without good reason that William Harvey published in Frankfurt his epoch-making dissertation *De motu cordis*, in which he proved the circulatory movement of the blood and thereby established modern physiology. Frankfurt was even more important as the seat of the largest European type-foundry. Founded in 1531 by Christian Egenolff and from 1629 known as the Luther foundry, the firm supplied types to every European (and later also American) printing establishment.

Frankfurt was also prominent among the places from which periodical publications went out to slake the ever-increasing thirst of the public for topical information. The first European newspapers, as distinct from the older newsbooks, were the

*Avisa*, published in Wolfenbüttel from 1609 and directed and partly written by Duke Heinrich Julius of Brunswick, a counsellor at the Prague court of Rudolf II, and therefore containing much first-hand political intelligence. In the same year, a Strasbourg printer started a *Relation* and in 1610 a 'Memorable Newspaper' began to appear in Cologne. Dutch publishers and journalists were the most enterprising; from 1618 onward they produced newspapers in Dutch, French and English; and much can be gathered about the wars in Germany from the English newspapers which two London stationers brought out from 1621 to 1632 when the Court of Star Chamber suppressed them because of their anti-Spanish and anti-Austrian bias; when the ban was lifted in 1638 these *Corantos* immediately reappeared.

Out of the mass of ephemeral newssheets and more or less regular newspapers which continued to appear throughout the Thirty Years War, two publications enjoyed the favour of a more serious-minded class of readers: the half-yearly *Relationis historicae semestralis continuatio* (from 1618) and the annual *Theatrum Europaeum* (from 1633), both published in Frankfurt. The *Theatrum* was founded by Matthäus Merian and during its hundred years of publication served the German public in a similar way as did later on Edmund Burke's *Annual Register*.

Journalists in the seventeenth century were as avid as their modern successors to seek out and, if need be, invent thrilling stories with which to titillate their readers and to increase the circulation of their papers. The morbid tales of cannibalism never fail to appeal to popular historians and novelists, as the surest proofs of the moral degeneracy into which the 'Thirty Years War' plunged Germany. The records of the few cases of alleged cannibalism which have been tried, are buried in the files of minor county courts. It can be taken for certain that only one case of genuine cannibalism has been established. During the long siege of Breisach by Bernard of Weimar (5 June to 17 December 1638) some famished soldiers of the imperial garrison were reduced to such an extremity that they ate the flesh of their dead comrades. A second case of what looks like cannibalism was proven in a Silesian court in 1653. The defendant, a highwayman, was convicted of the murder of some 250 persons over a period of eleven years. Among his victims was a pregnant woman, and the robber was accused of having eaten the heart of the unborn child. His confession, that he did it 'in order to make him more fierce and dreaded', disposes of the classification of this crime as cannibalism – every anthropologist will immediately recognize it as a clear case of superstitious magic, quite unconnected with any fear of starvation.

Tales of cannibalism, themselves journalistic stunts, snowballed easily into accepted truths. The *Theatrum Europaeum* reported that 'conditions in and around Worms' were so bad that the people were forced to eat human flesh; this tale, in the hands of a nineteenth-century historian, has been extended to cover 'for example' the districts of 'Saxony, Fulda, Hessen, along the Rhine and Alsace'. The prize for the most sweeping statement should perhaps go to another contributor to the *Theatrum*; it incidentally shows that German journalists pretended to some world-wide coverage. In 1639 he concluded a selection of improbable – and quite unsubstantiated – stories with the rhetorical question: 'Has Germany become America? Cannibals, previously known only by name, now openly walk about on the banks of the Rhine, the ancient seat of civilization.'

Whereas these examples show cannibalism as a means to satisfy unhealthy cravings for atrocity stories, a discreet hint at such disgusting practices could also be turned to rousing charitable emotions. A Calvinist preacher in the Palatinate sent out a circular letter to his brethren abroad asking for gifts to support his flock; in it, he used the sentimental metaphor that 'the food shortage is so great that the dead are no longer safe in their graves'. The success of this appeal was so effective that henceforth no writer of a begging-letter omitted a reference to body-snatching and cannibalism, without of course ever supplying factual evidence.

In short, cannibalism has to be struck from our history books, as have the colossal losses of population, the complete economic ruin, the collapse of civilization and all the other myths of the 'Thirty Years War'.

# Bibliographical Notes

THE following notes are not meant to take the place of a bibliography of the Thirty Years War. They aim to direct the attention of the student to some recent publications which the author has found particularly helpful.

The first historian to see the Thirty Years War in its European setting rather than as a German affair was Georges Pagès, *La Guerre de Trente Ans* (Paris, 1939; 2nd ed., 1949). The only modern work in English is C. V. Wedgwood, *The Thirty Years War* (London, 1938; Pelican reprint, 1957), but it is vitiated by taking a narrow, sentimental German view.

The standard work in German, Moriz Ritter, *Deutsche Geschichte im Zeitalter der Gegenreformation und des Dreissigjährigen Krieges* (3 vols, Stuttgart, 1889–1908) has become obsolete. The latest large-scale book, Günther Franz, *Der dreissigjährige Krieg und das deutsche Volk* (Jena 1940), is tainted by the author's Nazi proclivities. Surprisingly, the best 'history' in the German language is a novel, or rather a vast tapistry of tableaux, composed with exceptional psychological insight by a novelist and poet who was a trained historian: Ricarda Huch, *Der grosse Krieg in Deutschland* (3 vols, Leipzig, 1914).

A stimulating selection from the writings of some twenty German, French, English, American, Swedish and Czech historians is given in *The Thirty Years War: Problems of Motive, Extent and Effect*, ed. Theodore K. Rabb (Boston, Mass., 1964).

*Background. The New Cambridge Modern History*, vol. IV (scheduled for publication in 1967).

*France and Spain.* H. Hauser, *La Prépondérance espagnole, 1559–1660* (Paris, 1933); B. Chudoba, *Spain and the Empire, 1519–1643* (Chicago, 1952); G. Mecenseffy, *Die Beziehungen der Höfe von Wien und Madrid während des Dreissigjährigen Krieges* (Archiv für österr. Geschichte, 121, 1955); Georges Pagès, *Naissance du Grand Siècle* (Paris, 1948).

*Netherlands.* P. Geyl, *The Netherlands in the 17th Century*, vol. I (London, 1961).

*Russia.* O. L. Vainstein, *Rossiya i Tridsatyilyetnyaya Voyna* (Moscow, 1947).

*The Bohemian-Palatine War.* J. Polišenský, *Anglie a Bílá Hora* (Prague, 1949) and *Nizozemská Politika a Bílá Hora* (Prague, 1958); G. Mecenseffy, *Geschichte des Protestantismus in Oesterreich* (Vienna, 1956).

*The struggle for the Grisons.* A. Pfister, *Georg Jenatsch, sein Leben und seine Zeit* (2nd ed., Basel, 1939).

*The Danish War.* H. D. Loose, *Hamburg und Christian IV von Dänemark* (Hamburg, 1963); V. Vilar, *Un gran proyecto anti-holandés* (Hispania 88, 1962).

*The Mantuan Succession.* R. Quazza, *La guerra per la successione di Mantova e del Monferrato* (2 vols., Mantua, 1926).

*The Swedish War.* M. Roberts, *Gustavus Adolphus: A History of Sweden, 1611–32.* 2 vols. (London, 1953–58); the only completely satisfactory biography of any personality of the period.

*Wallenstein.* After a century of painstaking research Leopold Ranke, *Geschichte Wallensteins* (Berlin, 1869) has remained the classical 'biography which expands into history', as the author explained his aim. The final catastrophe has been treated by the Czech historian Josef Pekař, *Valdšteyn* (Prague, 1934; German translation, Berlin, 1937) and the Austrian historian H. von Srbik, *Wallensteins Ende* (2nd ed., Salzburg, 1952). A. Ernstberger, *Wallenstein als Volkswirt im Herzogtum Friedland* (Prague, 1929) and *Hans de Witte, Finanzmann Wallensteins* (Wiesbaden, 1954), deal with Wallenstein's economic policy.

*The Franco-Swedish Conflict with Austria-Spain.* H. Kellenbenz, *Hamburg und die französisch–schwedische Zusammenarbeit im Dreissigjährigen Krieg* (Zeitschrift des Vereins für Hamburgische Geschichte, 49/50, 1964).

*The Peace of Westphalia.* Fritz Dickmann, *Der Westfälische Frieden* (2nd ed., Münster, 1965), a standard work for the whole period of 1630–48; M. Braubach, *Der Westfälische Friede* (Münster, 1948), the best short study.

*The Franco-Spanish War.* G. Marañon, *El Conde-Duque de Oliváres* (3rd ed., Madrid, 1952), slightly romanticized.

*Myth and Reality.* R. Ergang, *The Myth of the all-destructive fury of the Thirty Years War* (Pocono Pines, Pa., 1956), has amassed and condensed (in 40 pages) a vast amount of information; the bibliography lists many out-of-the-way books and papers.

*Military Aspects.* Hans Delbrück, *Geschichte der Kriegskunst im Rahmen der politischen Geschichte.* vol. 4 (Berlin, 1920); standard work. E. von Frauenholz, *Entwicklungsgeschichte des deutschen Heerwesens*, vol. III (Berlin, 1938).

*Economic Aspects.* D. V. Glass and D. E. C. Eversley, *Population in History* (London, 1965); J. A. van Houtte, *Onze zeventiende eeuw 'Ongelukseeuw'?* (Mededelingen Koninglijke Vlaamse Academie, 15, 1953); E. Woehlkens, *Pest und Ruhr im 16. Jahrhundert* (Uelzen, 1954); K. F. Olechnowitz, *Handel und Seeschiffahrt der späten Hanse* (Weimar, 1965); P. Jeannin, *Les comptes du Sund* (Revue historique, 231, 1964).

*Cultural Life.* E. Rose, *A History of German Literature* (New York, 1960); chapter V gives an all-round picture of the intellectual background of the period.

# Index

Political and denominational units – such as France, Germany, Netherlands, Spain, Sweden, Calvinism, Lutherans, Roman Church, or their equivalents (Habsburg, Holy Roman Empire, United Provinces, etc.) – have not been listed as they occur on virtually every, or every other, page.